The Craft of Revision

Donald M. Murray

Holt, Rinehart, and Winston, Inc.
Fort Worth   Chicago   San Francisco   Philadelphia
Montreal   Toronto   London   Sydney   Tokyo

Publisher Ted Buchholz
Acquisitions Editor Michael A. Rosenberg
Senior Project Editors Dawn Youngblood
                          Christine Caperton
Copyeditor Linda Buchanan Allen
Production Manager Kathleen Ferguson
Art & Design Supervisor / Text Serena Barnett
Text Designer Paula Goldstein
Art & Design Supervisor / Cover Vicki McAlindon Horton
Cover Designer Marisa Dilley

Library of Congress Cataloging-in-Publication Data
Murray, Donald Morrison, 1924–
    The craft of revision / Donald M. Murray.
    Includes index.
    1. English language—Rhetoric. 2. Editing. I. Title.
PE1408.M787   1991   808'.042—dc20   90-43196

"The Digging" from *Death of a Naturalist* by Seamus Heaney.
Reprinted with permission of Faber and Faber Ltd.

ISBN: 0-03-070692-0

Requests for permission to make copies of any part of the work should be mailed to: Copyrights and Permissions Department, Holt, Rinehart and Winston, Inc., Orlando, FL 32887. Address editorial correspondence to 301 Commerce Street, Suite 3700, Fort Worth, TX 76102. Address orders to 6277 Sea Harbor Drive, Orlando, FL 32887, 1-800-782-4479 or 1-800-433-0001 (in Florida).

Printed in the United States of America
1 2 3 4   016   9 8 7 6 5 4 3 2

Holt, Rinehart and Winston, Inc.
The Dryden Press
Saunders College Publishing

for Minnie Mae
who made soup of old bones
and mailed out manuscripts
in which I had no faith

To the Instructor

"Revise," we command, and our students change some of the punctuation, often trading new grammatical errors for old; choose a couple of long words they don't really know from Roget to "profound it up" as one of my students said; misspell a number of words in a more innovative way; catch a few typos, and pass back essentially the same paper.

It is all they know.

And it was all I knew until, after I had worked for newspapers for six years, I learned the craft of magazine and book writing. The first work I did in studying the writing process focused on revision; now, years later, I have returned to the craft of revision.

Writing Is Rewriting

At our desks, writers make writing work. We take the rare gifts of inspiration, usually as wonderful and ugly as a new-born baby, and nurture them so they grow into essay, poem, novel, textbook, review, report, whatever is their destiny. And when we don't have inspiration, which is most of the time, we know how to produce a first draft we can work—by revision—into a final, publishable draft.

We know that revision is not punishment; that writing evolves from a sequence of drafts, each one teaching the writer how to write the next one. And we know that revision is copy editing and much, much more.

Scientists know that failure is essential, central, and necessary to their trade. They experiment and from the experiments that don't work—most of them—they discover the questions they need to ask, the method of asking them, and eventually, some answers. They revise.

Actors and musicians rehearse. Retailers test markets, politicians take polls, manufacturers try pilot runs. They all revise, and so do writers. *Writing is rewriting.*

The Craft of Revision

Writing is a decision-making process. As we revise, considering each word, each piece of punctuation, each phrase, sentence, paragraph, page, we make decisions that lead to other decisions. We don't work by intuition but by craft.

This text takes the student into the workshop—into the head—of one publishing writer while writing is being made through revision. There are differences among the way writers work and this is taken into account, based on my study of how writers write that I began in junior high school. The text reveals the attitudes and the skills of the revising writer.

It is interesting that both good students and poor ones are equally unable to revise. The best students fall in love with their first drafts, and when they make them superficially correct they think they are finished; the poorest students also look to the mysteries of presentation—spelling, handwriting, mechanics, usage—and see nothing beyond that. But revision is based on re-seeing the entire piece of writing.

This book shows the student how to create a discovery draft and then how to read the draft to see what has been discovered. Then the text takes the student through the decisions of revision: focus, audience, form, information, structure, and language. They are dealt with in an orderly, sequential manner that the student can adapt to a variety of writing tasks.

The student has a writer companion who helps the student read and revise the student's own draft until it communicates the draft's own meaning with clarity and grace.

What Will Make
Students Want To Revise?

The writer's motivation to revise comes from a positive and a negative force—and so will the student's. The positive force is the surprise of discovery. Writers are born at the moment they write what they do not expect and find a potential significance in what is on the page. They add a word or two, cut a few, move the others around, and watch that potential meaning come clear. They are hooked because the act of writing that, in the past, had revealed their ignorance, now reveals that they know more than they thought they knew, had more to say than they had realized.

Now they can understand what Hemingway meant when he said, "Prose is architecture not interior decoration." The students had thought that revising was only a superficial—to them—matter of etiquette and neatness, a dressing up of a message to which they had no commitment. Now they have a message they want heard and understood by readers. They are ready to be motivated by the negative force of reader understanding.

Students recognize that they need the craft of clarity and the craft of grace. To be read and understood they must know the traditions of language and break them only when it results in increased clarity. They have to meet the reader's expectations and find a common ground on which they can communicate.

Rewriting is, above all, a matter of attitude. And the teacher must model an attitude that emphasizes discovery and then communication. The teacher who says, "We all hate to rewrite but . . ." will breed a class that hates rewriting. The teacher who knows firsthand the excitement of revision, and may even share examples of personal revision, may make an interest in revision contagious.

How Can Students
Learn the Craft of Revision?

Students, first of all, must learn a positive attitude toward revision, which has usually been taught as punishment. The process of revision, for most students, has not been concerned with finding meaning, but has focused on editing superficial mechanical and grammatical errors to a preconceived and often not clearly understood standard. It is important for students to see revision in a larger context that *includes* editing, but is *not only* a matter of editing.

Some ways that the students' context can be expanded in the composition class include:

- First readings by the student writer, the instructor, and classmates should focus on potential, not error.
- There should be time for revision. Usually this means fewer papers, revised more extensively.
- The best as well as the worst papers should have the benefits of revision.
- Students should observe the discoveries of meaning made clear by revision on classmates' papers as well as their own.
- The process of revision should be sequential, moving from a concern with meaning through audience, form, information, structure, to language.

Above all, attitude motivates the learning of skills. The instructor should reinforce a constructive attitude toward revision. Some of the ways this can be done are:

- Share evolving drafts that document the positive results of revision. Reveal the instructor's own revision case histories, have students who have revised effectively share their own case histories, share the case histories of successful revision from interviews and biographies of writers.
- Have class members and possibly faculty members from other disciplines report on activities in their disciplines that are similar to revision: dramatic and musical rehearsal, practice in a sport, the process of painting, experiments in science.
- Have the class perform quick revisions, for example, writing a five-line description of a familiar place or person in five

minutes, then do five-minute rewrites from a different point of view, for a different purpose, for a different audience, in a different form, in a different voice, and share the results so the class appreciates the diverse products of revision.

At each stage of the revision process, students should play with the skills of shifting focus, appealing to different audiences, experimenting with form, manipulating information, restructuring, turning the draft's voice.

Six Ways To Use the Craft of Revision in Your Classroom

This text has been designed to support the student and instructor in many different courses. It can be used alone or as a supplement to other rhetorics and readers. Teachers will and should find their own ways to adapt this text to their particular teaching style, the needs of their own students, and the curriculum in which they function. These suggestions are designed to spark the diversity that should be central to teaching writing.

1. *The Craft of Revision* can be used as the principal writing text since it helps the student create a first draft. The students can use it to help them write weekly papers, or it can be used to support a sequence of three-week units in which the student writes a draft and performs two major revisions supported by conferences, peer workshops, and class instruction sessions. I have had good results with students working on one paper all semester, taking several weeks to find the subject, then moving week-by-week through the revision process. They didn't get bored because they found subjects they wanted to explore. In fact, class-alumni response has been unusually strong, saying they really learned to write when they had time to learn the craft of revision.

2. This text can supplement a rhetoric that has limited material on revision, or it can supplement a reader, allowing the students to understand the craft that created the models and to practice the same craft on their own drafts.

3. *The Craft of Revision* can be introduced to the class in the first week or two and then used as a reference book by the

xii   To the Instructor

students as they revise their papers. The best way to do this is to have the students write a paragraph in class, then revise it a number of times, sharing each revision with a small group who will select the most interesting leap towards meaning to share with the whole class.

The students may need to be told in the beginning what to do, since they have only been told to edit in the past. I usually say, "Develop the potential in your draft, exploring the subject in writing any way you want, but if you're stuck you may want to change the point of view from which the subject is seen."

Some other suggestions I may make are: try to make the information more specific, revise it for a different publication or audience, write with more emotion or less, try to write in a different voice.

The writing periods should be short, no more than five minutes, and the peer sharing session no longer than fifteen minutes. It always helps if the instructor performs the same exercise and shares those drafts. Once the students experience the discovery that is possible with revision, they can be introduced to the text.

4. The text may be used in the latter half of a composition semester or term when the students have drafts worthy of careful revision and when they see the need for revision.

5. The text may be used in a content course in English or any other discipline to help the students improve their writing assignments. The text may be assigned to all students in the course or suggested as an aid to those students who are having difficulty revising effectively.

6. *The Craft of Revision* can be used as a self-teaching text with the student creating a draft and moving through the sequential steps to practice the skills of revision.

In every case the students should use the text in connection with their own writing. The craft of revision cannot be learned in the abstract; theory must be illuminated by practice that will, in turn, illuminate theory.

And however the text is used it will help the individual student, the instructor, and the whole class if those students who do an effective job of revision testify to the class on what they did and how. Sharing will reinforce the student and instruct everyone else. I have done this with oral reports but more recently with quickly written but complete commentaries that the students write, reporting on their writing and revision process, their writing problems and their proposed solutions. These commentaries encourage students to examine their craft and teach the student how they can identify and solve their own writing problems. And these solutions instruct us all.

My students have always instructed me, and I have told worried, inexperienced writing teachers to get their students writing. In every class, some students write better than others. Get them to tell you and the class how they wrote and the curriculum will evolve.

Acknowledgments

Every book has its own history of indebtedness but this book has a number of people to whom I am especially grateful.

My wife, Minnie Mae, is my first reader and most demanding critic. Chip Scanlan, my closest writing friend, is always as near as the telephone.

The book was the idea of Charlyce Jones Owen and that idea was cultivated in an especially creative way by Michael Rosenberg who has been a skillful, thoughtful editor who helped me see what was written rather than what we intended to write.

Dr. Mary Clark of the English Department at the University of New Hampshire is an expert linguist and a fine teacher who has helped me understand—and usually follow—the traditions of language. She should receive credit for what you like that I practice and say about language, but none of the blame for my eccentricities. She has been a knowledgeable, patient, and candid critic of each line in this text.

Dr. Brock Dethier and soon-to-be Dr. Bonnie Sunstein are colleagues and friends who gave my first draft extraordinarily close and constructive criticism when they were burdened by their own crowded schedules. I had their criticism and support when it was crucial.

I was also instructed by the honest, detailed responses of others who read my first draft:

Driek Zirinsky, Boise State University; Ernest Lee, Carson-Newman College; Joan Tyler Mead, Marshall University; Kathleen L. Bell, Old Dominion University; and Marie B. Czarnecki, Mohawk Valley Community College.

As usual, the editorial staff, designers and editors at Holt, Rinehart and Winston have earned my respect and gratitude: Dawn Youngblood and Christine Caperton, senior project editors; Linda Buchanan Allen, free-lance copyeditor; Laurie Runion, editorial assistant; Kathleen Ferguson, production manager; Serena Barnett, design supervisor/text; and Vicki McAlindon Horton, design supervisor/cover.

Contents

To the Instructor   vii

1
Writing Is Rewriting   1

The Satisfactions of Revision   3
The Craft of Revision   10
The Process of Revision   11
Putting the Revision Process to Work   15
Demonstrating the Writing Process   17

2
Draft to Explore   23

The Explorer's Attitude   26
What Am I Looking for?   28
How Do I Explore in Writing?   31
Where Do I Explore?   39
How Do I Start Exploring?   42
How Do I Keep Exploring?   47

3
Read to Discover   49

Reading as a Reader   49
Reading for Discovery   51
What Works?   55
What Needs Work?   59

4
Revise for Meaning   64

Say One Thing   65
Frame Your Meaning   68
Set the Distance   70
The Importance of Focus   72

5
Revise for Audience   73

Identify Your Reader   74
Re-create Your Reader's World   75
Ask Your Reader's Questions   79
Use Test Readers   80

6
Revise for Order   86

Discovering the Form of the Draft   87
Design Your Own Form   97
Keeping in; Cutting out   102
Discovering Your Structure   104
Designing an Effective Structure   108

7
Revise for Evidence 112

The Importance of Information 112
The Qualities of Effective Information 114
Basic Forms of Information 119
Where Do You Find Information? 120
Writing Information 128

8
Revise for Voice 132

Hearing Your Voice 132
Tuning the Voice of the Draft 142
The Craft of Revision 147

9
Rewriting Is Writing 174

Rewriting Before Writing 174
Rewriting While Writing 177

Index 179

The Craft of Revision

1

Writing Is Rewriting

The myth: The writer sits down, turns on the faucet, and writing pours out—clean, graceful, correct, ready for the printer.

The reality: The writer gets something—anything—down on paper, reads it, tries it again, rereads, rewrites, again and again.

For years I denied the reality. I held firm to three beliefs:

- First draft was best. Good writing was spontaneous writing.
- Rewriting was punishment for failure. The editor or teacher who required revision was a bad reader who had no respect for my spontaneous writing.
- Revision was a matter of superficial correction that forced my natural style to conform to an old-fashioned, inferior style.

No one challenged my literary theology; editors simply didn't publish my writing. And I needed to get published. I wanted to eat.

Bob Johnson of the *Saturday Evening Post,* then the leading free-lance market, liked what was in an article of mine. He said they would hire a writer to fix it up.

"I'm a writer," I said confidently.

"Well," he said doubtfully.

"I want to write it myself," I pleaded. "Please," I begged.

He sent me a single-spaced letter of criticism that was longer than the article I had submitted. I rewrote, and then rewrote what I rewrote. He traveled from Philadelphia to Boston to go over my revision word-by-word, line-by-line. Again I rewrote—and rewrote.

The article was published and editors on other magazines spent time teaching me the craft of revision despite the guer-rilla war of resistance I fought line-by-line.

I rewrote. I wanted to be published; I needed to eat. I still felt, however, that I failed when I had to revise my first draft. I thought real writers had that faucet they could turn on. I thought I was a poor writer who had to rewrite to be published.

Then I began to listen to what my editors and the publish-ing writers I met told me: Revision is a normal and essential part of the editorial process. I started to pay attention to—and be comforted by—the testimony of hundreds of the best writers of past and present:

> Because the best part of all, the absolutely most delicious part, is finishing it and then doing it over . . . . I rewrite a lot, over and over again, so that it looks like I never did.
>
> TONI MORRISON

> I've done as many as twenty or thirty drafts of a story. Never less than ten or twelve drafts.
>
> RAYMOND CARVER

> My writing is a process of rewriting, of going back and chang-ing and filling in.
>
> JOAN DIDION

> When I see a paragraph shrinking under my eyes like a strip of bacon in a skillet, I know I'm on the right track.
>
> PETER deVRIES

> What makes me happy is rewriting.
>
> ELLEN GOODMAN

> Rewriting is when playwriting really gets to be fun. In baseball you only get three swings and you're out. In rewriting, you get

almost as many swings as you want and you know, sooner or later, you'll hit the ball.

NEIL SIMON

I love the flowers of afterthought.

BERNARD MALAMUD

I began to hear the message: *writing is rewriting.*

The Satisfactions of Revision

Slowly, almost without realizing it, and certainly without admitting it to any editor, I became addicted to revision. I found rewriting seductive. I saw—draft by draft—unexpected but significant meanings come clear; I heard—line-by-line—the music of my voice adapted to the purpose of the text.

Before, the first draft was that terrible combination of ambition and terror. I wanted to write the great story, article, poem, the one that had never been written before, the one that would establish a new standard for perfection.

And having set that impossible goal, I suffered—appropriately—fear raised to terror, anxiety multiplied by apprehension. But once I got something down, forced by deadline and hunger, I was not suspended between absolute perfection and total failure. I had a draft I could read and develop; I could roll up my sleeves and get to work.

Problems to Solve

I learned to be grateful because revision revealed problems to be solved and we are ultimately problem-solving animals. I had problems of subject, of meaning, of organization, of communication, of language. And the identified problem, exposed and defined by rereading and rewriting, usually presents possible solutions.

Oh, this piece of writing is terrible, awful, awful terrible, I can't write. Moan. Whimper. Wail. Sob. You've heard others; you've heard yourself; I've heard myself.

But rereading and rewriting lead you out of the swamp of self-pity. Now you can identify the problems, one at time.

"This paper on the Great Depression is a mess," says the writer to the writer.

"OK, but what kind of a mess?"

"I've got a lot of facts. Unemployment. The market. Stuff like that. Good stuff but it's all a jumble."

"What do you mean, a jumble?"

"There's no order. It isn't lined up. The reader wouldn't see the, what do you call it, sequence, the way one thing leads to another, the process that makes a depression inevitable. That's my point."

"Good. Now you know what to do."

"What?"

"Think about it. How do you make the sequence clear?"

"Maybe an outline. Perhaps subheads. An introduction that says what I'm trying to prove, then the steps to prove it, then a conclusion."

"Sounds good. Try it."

Inexperienced writers can solve, by common sense and their experience in other fields, most writing problems, and that process is satisfying. Most of us feel good when we solve a problem.

Exploration

The hard work of revision was fascinating because I was not correcting my copy, I was exploring my subject. Before the first draft I felt dumb. Now as I rewrote I discovered how much I knew. The writing gave me questions to ask, trails to explore.

Writing leads to more writing. Topics grow and split, increasing the subjects I have to write about. People ask me where I get my ideas—mostly from my writing. I explore one subject and see many others to explore. And I like the process of exploration—learning—that takes place when I rewrite and re-rewrite.

Discovery

Exploration leads to discovery and that is my principal motivation to write and rewrite. I surprise myself on the page. I do not write what I intend but what I had no intent of writing. There is always new territory I can perceive through the draft, new mountain ranges, great tidal inlets, cities, ships on the horizon of a type I have never seen.

I used to worry that there would be no new discoveries for me in writing. A day would come when the magic would be gone. I no longer worry about that. I have been publishing for more than fifty years and yet, each morning at my desk, I am fifteen years old and the world is new. In fact, I have learned to be freer in my writing, to take more risks to explore close to—and beyond—the edge.

As I have learned the craft of revision, I have learned how to see the discoveries that used to lie hidden before my eyes. And through this same craft, I am able to develop those discoveries so I am saying more than I could have hoped to say when I began the draft. Sometimes the discoveries are large—this was not a book on revision when I began it—and others are small— the word *companioned,* which does not yet appear in the dictionary, is just right for a line of poetry I have written:

> Now I live most alone with others, companioned
> by silence and the long road at my back,
> mirrored by daughters . . .

Each of the discoveries is satisfying in its own way; each contains a surprise and there is something on the page that was not there before. I have the feeling of accomplishment someone else gets from lifting a fresh loaf of bread from the oven, slowly playing in a rainbow trout, sinking a three-pointer, building a shelf that is true and strong.

Memory

I have a poor memory until I write. The act of writing brings back—in context—the revealing details of childhood in the 1920s, combat in the 1940s, high school in the 1930s, the police-headquarters press room in 1950, the night I spent alone on Uncle Don's boat in 1943, the abandoned village I "discovered" in the New Hampshire woods in 1938, the intensive-care ward in which my daughter died in 1977, the trip I took in the Scandinavian Arctic in 1989, the summer I learned to swim, 1936.

If I were to write about any of those events, I would recover from that enormous memory bank in my brain sights, sounds, smells, tastes, phrases; I would see actions and reactions; recover feelings and thoughts I had at the time. And I will remember many things I never knew I observed and stored away, for my brain is recording more than I am aware of at any moment, including this one.

Rewriting mobilizes these resources within the brain, makes them worthwhile as the act of writing gives them meaning. I don't know what I remember—and its importance—until I start a draft and see before me a rediscovered world.

Awareness

I am never bored because I am always writing and rewriting in my head and in my daybook. I am an observer of my own life, a scholar of what I feel and see and hear and care about. I tend to my anger and my sense of humor; I try to make sense of the life I am living and the lives that surround me.

Rewriting multiplies my awareness. Sitting in a traffic jam, I watch those who talk and sing to themselves or act out scenes in which they, at last, tell off the boss as if they had privacy in a car. Waking at night and having trouble going back to sleep, I revise yesterday's pages in my head. Sitting in the parking lot, I try to describe shoppers' walks and make mental notes on how each walk reveals anxiety, satisfaction, despair, pleasure, love, hate. Sitting in a boring meeting or class, I take my daybook and revise a poem, a paragraph, the opening of an article—or the ending.

And when what I observe seems predictable, I ask the question Bob Cormier, a wonderfully inventive writer, asks: "What if?" What if the butcher took the cleaver and . . . . What if that housewife took the groceries and drove to Dayton, Ohio . . . . What if the fifty-year-old man in the three-button suit leaned over and kissed the high-school-aged supermarket sacker girl putting the groceries in the station wagon . . . . What if she were his daughter—his daughter that had been placed for adoption at birth; his baby sitter; his partner's daughter; his child bride; his . . . . What if, what if, what if?

My awareness on the page increases my awareness when I am not writing; my awareness of my world, of myself reacting to that world, increases my awareness when I am writing. This circle of awareness increases the richness of my life.

Connection

The information we collect connects, almost on its own, with other information. It seems driven to make meaning. Revision connects fragments of information that we thought were unrelated. And it is from these unexpected relationships that new meanings are born. In writing, two and seven and a bag of fresh chocolate-chip cookies add up to four. A quotation, an image, a statistic, a feeling that seem unrelated reveal an unexpected meaning when they meet in a draft.

The writer rewriting is a magnet for information. Facts, observations, ideas, citations, actions performed and actions unperformed, answers, questions all are collected and then, in the rewriting, join in producing insight, conclusion, theory, idea, thesis, proof.

Pattern

Marge Piercy made me see anew the profound importance of pattern when she said:

> I think that the beginning of fiction, of the story, has to do with the perception of pattern in event, of the large rhythms in things like birth, growth, decline and death, and the short rhythms like the excitement of searching for things and finding them, the repetition of the sexual pattern, these are things that we experience again and again as having dramatic shape. At the basis of fiction is a desire to find meaningful shape in events, in the choices people make.

And this is just as true of nonfiction, history essay and lab report, term paper and blue-book exam, book review and paper of literary criticism. It is pattern that reveals and contains meaning.

The biologist looks through the microscope, the astronomer looks through the telescope, the accountant through the spread sheet, the historian through colonial records, the coach through the team's stats, the writer through the draft, all seeking patterns that reveal meaning, that carry within them implication.

Music

One of the great enjoyments of rewriting is that it allows me to hear the music of what I read, the music of others and the music of my own drafts, at first faint, and then with tuning, strong and clear.

Voice is most likely the element that keeps you reading, that makes you care about what is being said, that makes you trust the writer. The music—or voice of the text—underlies and supports the meaning of what you have to say and it is the music from my first draft that tells me the meaning of what I have written. As I listen to the music of the draft, I begin to understand the meaning of the text and as I hear how it will sound in the reader's ear I learn how to revise for that reader so the meaning will be heard.

There is enormous satisfaction in revising or tuning the music of a draft. Change the word, the pauses between words, the beat, the length of the line, all the elements that communicate the music of the text, and the message of the text comes clear.

Communication

A benefit of revision is communication. Heather McHugh said, "I began to write because I was too shy to talk, and too lonely not to send messages." Writing is an antidote to loneliness.

I was—am—shy. As a child I hid in the closet when company came; now I say I am out of town when the invitation to the cocktail party arrives. But by writing I found that what Kafka said—"A book should serve as the axe for the frozen sea within us"—was true.

I write and meet readers—you—whom I have never seen, will probably never see. I play in many games as a writer. For example, I dropped out of high school twice, then flunked out in part because I thought the way writing was taught was stupid.

Now through writing, I have had my say about how writing should be taught and have earned the "compliment" of having those who taught the way I was taught calling my methods stupid. But now I am not a disenfranchised drop-out, I am an empowered participant and although not everyone, thank goodness, shares my views, they all hear them because I have revised and revised them until they can be heard.

The Adventure of Thought

I am fascinated by spiders—at a distance. They weave their webs of their own lives it seems and I think I weave in language the meanings of my own life. Plato said, "The life which is unexamined is not worth living." I agree and I have examined and re-examined my life by writing.

Rewriting is thinking. There is satisfaction in making meaning of what has happened to you, what is happening to you, integrating reading, study, research, observation, feeling, reaction until you come up with some possible answers—and some good, tough questions that need more thinking and rethinking.

Writing is the most disciplined form of thinking; writing is the fundamental tool of the intellectual life. Write your life down and you can stand back and study it, learn from it. Writing demands precision of language, logical structure, documentation, focus. Writing is a fascinating discipline of mind.

The Pleasure of Craft

Above all else, the act of revision is central to the pleasure of making. When we build a house, bake a batch of Christmas cookies, cut a cross-country ski trail through the woods, write an essay, we add to the world.

And in the making we lose ourselves. Writing is my hobby and my obsession. Before I sit down to write I put on a compact disc and turn up the volume, but when I become lost in the writing and rewriting I no longer hear the music or know if it stops; I forget the time, the place, who I am going to meet for lunch, what errands I will run that afternoon. I forget my worries, fears, problems when I am in the work. As

Bernard Malamud said, "If it is winter in the book, spring surprises me when I look up."

Do not minimize this gift. The joy—yes, joy—of crafting a text under my hand and with my ear is a daily satisfaction to me. I am so involved in the task that I achieve concentration and that is the reason we do those activities that give us the most pleasure. Casting for a trout, painting a picture or a house, building a shelf, creating a great soup, conducting an experiment in the lab, constructing an arterial bypass to the heart or to downtown, we are lost in the making. Our life achieves, for the moment, a healing concentration of effort.

These are a few of the satisfactions of revision. As a first-draft writer I stand back from the actual writing process. When I revise, I am totally involved. I am playing the game of making meaning with language and as someone who has played the games of football and hockey, the game of jumping out of airplanes, the terrible "game of war," I find rewriting the most exciting game of all.

The Craft of Revision

The craft of revision gives us experience within the writing act. Reading about writing—or being talked to about writing—tells us what the writing experience *may* be; reading written writing allows us to imagine what its writing *may* have been like; writing, reading, and revising allow us to experience the writing act. We go backstage and see how the printed text is made and learn the craft of revision that precedes publication. We learn to write by rewriting.

Each writing problem is not solved the same way. As we gain experience in revision, we build up a repertoire of solutions that we can try when we confront an old, familiar problem—or a new one.

Our attitude changes as we rewrite successfully. We do not see problems as obstacles but rather as opportunities. We are problem-solving animals and rewriting is the skill of solving written-language problems. When we realize that we can solve problems in our writing, that we have an inventory of solutions to try, and when we learn that we can combine and adapt, even improvise solutions, then writing becomes a game and we do not so much work as play.

And we begin to read in a different way, picking up new moves from pages written by others. Once we know the problems behind the page that are invisible to ordinary writers, we can begin to recognize when the writer faced those problems and be fascinated by their solution. Failure stops being failure. The solution that works and the one that does not work are both experiments in meaning and from the "failed" experiment we may learn how to try one that will work.

The Process of Revision

Revision is a logical process. The overwhelming task of revising an essay—or a book—is based on a sequence of decisions. Certain problems have to be solved before other problems. The sequence can be understood and adapted to the rewriter's way of thinking, working, and writing as well as to the particular writing task.

But to adapt it is necessary first to understand the basic process. This means that tasks that the experienced rewriter may do simultaneously have to be broken down for the inexperienced writer to understand and practice. There is a chapter on each of these stages in the revision process, but first it is important to have an overview of the complete process.

Draft to Explore

We can't rewrite until we have a draft that explores the territory where there may be a subject. The writer has to lower the standards that may cause paralysis and write a rough draft that moves across the territory. This draft may be close to free writing, usually when the writer has not thought much about the territory to be explored, or it may be focused and look like a finished draft, especially when the writer has thought critically about the subject over an extensive period of time.

This is a time for honesty: The first draft may be finished. Rewriting is not a virtue, it is an essential process—most of the time for most writers.

Read to Discover

After we have completed a draft we should read it not so much for what we intended to write but for what we did not intend to write. The act of writing is the act of thinking, and if we are lucky our page will move beyond our intentions. When I read my drafts, I read for surprise.

Sometimes I am aware of the surprise when I am drafting the text and follow it, developing its possibilities as I write. My reading allows me to stand back and consider the surprise: Is this what I want to say? Other times the surprise may be hidden in a turn of voice, an unexpected word or phrase, a trail of evidence I was not aware of as I wrote. These surprises must be spotted and their implications considered: Is this the road I want to travel in the next draft?

Usually there are both obvious and hidden surprises in the text. If I do not see them, the reader will and be confused. I must read and deal with them by elimination or development. The real mistake is to see the surprises as mistakes. The unexpected—what you said as different from what you planned to say—is not an error. It is what happens when we write. The act of writing reveals possibilities of thought and presentation. If I knew what I was going to say in advance of writing, I would not bother to write and rewrite.

Of course, you have the final word. During revision you decide what you want to say and how you want to say it, but I have learned that you disregard the direction the text wants to take at a price. The text leads and the wise writer follows it if possible.

Revise for Meaning

After the reading has revealed the primary meaning of your text, you revise to make that meaning clear. Effective writing has focus. Everything in the draft must lead to that meaning or follow it. It is usually a good idea to write that meaning down. Such a line may or may not be in the text but it will be a North Star to guide you through the revision.

Inexperienced writers usually plunge in when revising and start to correct the language. It is a waste of time to work on the language line-by-line unless the meaning is clear to the reader.

Doesn't this attention to one dominant meaning lead you to throw good stuff away? Yes, a good draft might be measured by the amount of good material that has to be discarded. A powerful, rich draft grows from abundant soil. Besides, you can save the discarded good stuff for another day.

Revise for Audience

Now that you know what you want to make clear through revision, you should stand back and read it as a reader will. Again, you must not read what you intended to have in the draft, but what is actually on the page and what will be in the reader's mind. Does the rewriter become a mind reader? Yes. You can train yourself to read your text as a stranger. My trick is to imagine a specific reader. I pick someone I know who is intelligent but ignorant of my subject and uninterested in knowing about it.

I often role play, walking around my desk the way that reader walks, trying to sit as that reader would sit, reading as that reader would read, hastily, with a critical eye. I mark up the draft as that reading tells me what needs to be added, what must be moved to anticipate the reader's questions, what needs to be developed, what needs to be cut.

Revise for Order

When I know what I want to say and to whom I want to say it, I can reconsider the shape and sequence of the draft.

First I have to consider the form or genre of the draft. Is it appropriate to the message and the message receiver? I may decide the memo needs to become a familiar letter or a more formal report; the book review may become a literary essay. And, of course, if the form is assigned and I have no choice, I must make sure that I know and respond to the readers' expectations when they confront that form. The distance the writer stands from the subject and the documentation the reader expects is not the same for a familiar letter as it is for a term paper.

When the form is established I can pay attention to the structure with the draft. Do my arguments anticipate the reader's responses and deal with them in the order they will occur to the reader? Do my points move forward in a logical sequence? Does the structure of the draft support my dominant meaning?

Revise for Evidence

Now that we know the focus, the reader, the form and structure, we must make sure that we have the evidence to support that meaning. We should not depend on one form of evidence but have as much variety as possible within the traditions of the genre in which we are writing.

Most of us fall into a pattern of documentation. I tend to use—and overuse—personal anecdotes; another writer almost always uses statistics; another uses scholarly quotations. We must develop an inventory of evidence so that we can choose the particular documentation that is appropriate to the meaning we are communicating and that will persuade the reader we are attempting to reach.

Revise for Voice

And now we come to the magic of voice—that element of writing that unites meaning, order, evidence, and reader. This final stage of the revision process includes editing and more; it involves following the traditions of language or breaking them for good reason; it involves listening to and tuning the voice of the text.

As we read the text word-by-word, line-by-line, we must make sure that each word, the spaces between the words, the punctuation, all the elements of language work in harmony, that they are accurate, clear, and graceful.

Working with voice is the ultimate satisfaction for writers as we sit at the workshop bench, messing with the basic materials of our craft. After working with voice we can understand what the historian Barbara Tuchman said:

> Nothing is more satisfying than to write a good sentence. It is
> no fun to write lumpishly, dully, in prose the reader must plod

through like wet sand. But it is a pleasure to achieve, if one can, a clear running prose that is simple yet full of surprises. This does not just happen. It requires skill, hard work, a good ear and continued practice, as much as it takes Heifetz to play the violin.

And it is a profound form of play.

Putting the Revision Process to Work

Remember that the experienced writer may perform some or all of these tasks simultaneously. I have broken them down into stages so they can be understood and practiced.

And remember that there may be no need to perform each stage of revision on every text. In one case the meaning may be clear and the evidence all in hand; in another case the meaning may be confused but once that is solved, the rest falls in place; another time all is pretty well set but the voice is stiff, awkward, inappropriate; and most of the revision involves working with language.

The process of revision may change with the writing task. A teacher in our local high school, Dick Tappen, recently asked me to visit his class. He said that many of his students thought there was *one* writing process, that they had to find *the* writing process and then stick with it. He suspected and I knew that I have many writing and rewriting processes and that my processes this year are not the same as a few years ago and will not be the same a few years from now, but I did not know just what they were and how many I had until I wrote them down in preparation for his class. Here they are:

Column for the Boston Globe:

- Find a line.
- Write draft fast, in about 45 to 75 minutes.
- Read, revise, and edit.
- Check spelling.
- Read by my wife, Minnie Mae.
- Edit in response to her suggestions.
- Read by *Globe* by my *Globe* editor, Evelynne Kramer.
- Tear up, revise, or edit as needed.

For a newsletter I produced as writing coach for the *Boston Globe*:

Writing on Writing

- Written in chunks over two to four days. Revision incorporated into the chunking process. The chunks are not written in the order in which they will appear in the final draft.
- Revised and edited by myself, then checked for spelling on the computer.
- Read by *Globe* editor, Gerald D'Alfonso.
- Revised and edited as needed.

Textbooks

- Brainstorm titles (fifty?). Pick one.
- Write chapter outline. Over and over and over again.
- Write preface that says what is different about this book or this edition.
- Send to editor and a few colleagues.
- Consult with them.
- Write subheads for a chapter.
- Fill in items that may appear under chapter headings.
- Write and rewrite subheads for the chapter.
- Look for line and write lead, the first paragraph or so.
- Fill in text under chapter subheads, adding, cutting, and revising subheads as I go.
- Check spelling and have Minnie Mae check each chapter. Share chapters with daughters and two friends.
- Submit book to editor, who sends it to readers for review.
- Consult and absorb reviews.
- Rewrite.
- Put in mail.
- Respond to copy editor.

Poetry

- Hear a line, write it in daybook.
- In a fragment of time, write a half-poem, half-prose chunk in daybook.
- Work as a poem in daybook—one to three (four? five?) times.
- When it looks like a poem, I type it into the computer, revising as I go. I usually paste these drafts in my daybook and revise by hand in fragments of time.

- Check spelling and have Minnie Mae check.
- Share with my poetry mentor, Mekeel McBride.
- Revise.
- Put in mail. (Acceptance rate: about the same as maple syrup, about 40–1.)

Novel

- Brainstorm titles. Pick one.
- I have outlined and I have just plunged in.
- Write each chapter by "layering," writing over each day what I have written before, combining drafting and revising.
- When a chapter is finished I check spelling and have Minnie Mae check, then send it to my daughters and Chip Scanlan, my closest writer friend, for response, support, and safe-keeping.
- Out in mail to agent.
- Absorb response from editor.
- Revise and edit.

I have no loyalties to any particular process and neither should you. All the processes I described are different from what I would have used several years ago. I keep teaching myself to write by writing. Each process is a response to a specific writing task. The process is influenced by the genre, my experience with the genre and the task, the writing conditions I currently find productive. You should develop your own writing and rewriting processes.

Demonstrating the Writing Process

I am going to demonstrate the revision process with a game I have often played in class, taking three-by-five cards and quickly going through the revision process, writing on each card for three to five minutes. The purpose is not to produce great writing, although I am always surprised by the texts some students produce under these artificial conditions. Some of these revised paragraphs may grow later into fully developed essays, others may not; no matter. The purpose of this revision game is to get the feel of the entire revision process before each stage is studied in detail.

I come to the task empty-headed: Let's see, what will I write about? Where did my life change, what were the turning points? Freshman year, at Tilton Junior College. After all these years I have to remind myself not to try to write great literature, just to get something down, something that *may* have potential. Here's the first three-by-five card:

Draft to Explore and Read to Discover

Freshman year. A second chance. Dropped out of high school twice, flunked out. Got good job on newspaper but everyone who had same job was forty-five, fifty. Was I trapped? Chance to play football. Mort Howell. Editorial. If I came back from war, I would be a writer. Church.

Forty-nine words. Just fragments, notes to myself, but what potential. Each line brings back memories: of my shame and anger at my failure in high school, my pride at succeeding at work, my fear I would be trapped in jobs I hated as my father was because of his limited education. How important it was to me to play football. Mort Howell, the second good teacher I had. (The first was six years earlier.) Being part of the generation who knew we were all going to war. The decision to become a writer; leaving my parents' church.

I stepped back, staggered by the memories, then asked the questions I find most helpful in this situation: What surprised me? What did I learn? What itches? What do I want to explore? I look at what I have written and decide to explore how it felt to have a second chance. ▪

Revise for Meaning

I was a born-again freshman. I had been bored in school but I thought I was stupid, school was not for me, and then I got the chance to play football for a junior college. I escaped the problems at home, my reputation at high school, had a chance to make it into the middle class.

■ This is just a quick exercise and I have to remind myself of that and read to see if I've been able to focus on the meaning of a second chance. I like the accident of "born-again freshman" but after it the writing is flat. But it seems to be moving toward a focus on why I needed a second chance. Now, who is my audience? Who do I want to write it for? I know that many different audiences may read it, but I need to target the principal audience so I can make sure I appeal to that reader. It could be the people who read my "Over Sixty" column in the *Boston Globe* and who would remember their own freshman year at college. It could be those over-sixties, like my wife, who were deprived of a college education. It could be those of you who are freshmen in college. More specifically, it could be those of you who are experiencing a second chance in college. ■

Revise for Audience

In 1942 I was a born-again freshman. Riding up to New Hampshire on the train, I realized that I could not solve my parents' problems. They had to live their lives and I had to live mine. I was scared at meeting new people and relieved. They didn't know I was stupid and had flunked out of high school. I felt the train was steaming right along to the middle class, someday I would have a single-family home, oil heat controlled by a thermostat, running hot water—if I survived the war.

■ OK. I realized I had to date this and I realized I limited the audience to those of us who went—or are going—to college to move up economically. My message becomes clearer: It can be done. This may interest others but I am speaking to those in my situation.

   The form is clear, a reflective essay looking back at a crucial moment in my life. Now I have to look at the order in which I present my information so it will move the reader forward toward a meaning. ■

Revise for Order

In 1942 I experienced one of those years in which my life changed. I was leaving home on a train, but it wasn't a troop train—not yet. I had escaped my parents' private war, I had escaped the job that led nowhere, I had escaped my reputation as a high-school dropout and flunkout. Because of a fluke I was headed to a junior college to play football and become a good student—but I wouldn't have believed you if you had told me I would lead the class.

■ It was a small class. This is fun. I got this lined up in chronological order and found I could jump ahead. This might develop into a piece. It might be an effective opening paragraph in which I explore what did happen to me that year and the reader might be interested as well.

I did add more specific evidence as I wrote that last draft but I want to go over it again and see if I need more documentation. I'll underline anything new I add so it will be clear. ■

Revise for Evidence

In 1942 I experienced one of those years in which my life changed. I was leaving home on a train, but it wasn't a troop train—not yet. I had escaped my parents' civil war fought with a terrible silence, I had escaped the job of tearing out and pasting up newspaper advertisements that led nowhere, I had escaped my reputation in North Quincy High School as an irregular drop by, dropout and, finally, flunkout. Because of a fluke I was headed to Tilton Junior College in New Hampshire to play right tackle and earn As. I wouldn't have believed you if you had told me I would lead the class.

■ As a general rule, I find out that if I am more specific the piece becomes more lively and more authoritative. How specific? It depends in the same way that how much garlic in the salad depends on the cook, the meal, the diner.

Now I can listen to the music of the text and tune it so that it supports the meaning of the piece. I'll show my cross-outs and again underline anything new so you can see my working with language. ■

Revise for Voice

In 1942 I ~~experienced one of those years in which my life changed. I was leaving home~~ left home and ~~traveled farther than even I expected, an eighteen-year-old swollen with ambition~~ traveled so far I would never be able to return, farther than even I, an eighteen-year-old swollen with ambition, could hope. ~~on a train, but~~ It wasn't a troop train—not yet. I ~~had~~ would escaped the ~~my parents'~~ civil war my parents fought with a their terrible silences,; I would escape their debts and false promises, the sheriff at the door, the house dark because the electric bill was not paid; I ~~had~~ would escaped the job of tearing out and pasting up newspaper advertisements that led nowhere,; I ~~had~~ would escaped my reputation in North Quincy High School as ~~an irregular drop by,~~ dropout and, finally, flunkout. Because of a fluke I was headed to Tilton Junior College in New Hampshire to play right tackle and earn As. I was drunk on hope but I wouldn't have believed you if you had told me I would lead the class.

■ Now I will copy it over so you—and I—can read it without the interference of the editing. ■

In 1942 I left home and traveled so far I would never be able to return, farther than even I, an eighteen-year-old swollen with ambition, could hope. It wasn't a troop train—not yet. I would escape the civil war my parents fought with their terrible silences; I would escape their debts and false promises, the sheriff at the door, the house dark because the electric bill was not paid; I would escape the job of tearing out and pasting up newspaper advertisements that led nowhere; I would escape my reputation in North Quincy High School as a dropout and, finally, flunkout. Because of a fluke I was headed to Tilton Junior College in New Hampshire to play right tackle and earn As. I was drunk on hope but I wouldn't have believed you if you had told me I would lead the class.

Is it finished? Only for now. It demonstrates how one paragraph changed as it passed through the revision process. Try it yourself. Don't copy me, follow your own drafts to see where they take you.

I hope this book will help you as you write in school and outside of school, writing as students, lawyers, engineers, poets, politicians, doctors, executives, government officials. I also hope that whenever you write and rewrite you will enjoy that same process of discovery that makes my rewriting exciting to me. I never know when I start a draft where I will go and how I will get there. I hope you will be as fortunate as you find out that writing is rewriting.

2

Draft to Explore

To learn the craft of revision, we must first create a text to revise; to produce a text worthy of revision, we must experience writing as an act of discovery. Writing is not prethinking packaged for a reader, but is the process of thinking itself. We have thoughts, and turning them into written language defines, develops, extends those thoughts; we write, when all is going well, more than we expected to write. In writing, we are surprised by what we have written.

Recently the sports editor of the *Boston Globe* asked me to write an opening-day piece on my first visit to Fenway Park to see the Red Sox play. It is always fun to do a nostalgic piece and I agreed immediately, but when I got up the next morning to write about Fenway Park I found I was not so much writing about the Red Sox but about my father:

> When I think back to my first visit to Fenway Park, and all the visits since, I think of my father, who had no childhood, and how the Red Sox were the one constant thread of communication in our lives.

█ I found I had two territories to explore: the father who had no childhood and the relationship of father and son. I included material on Fenway Park and who played for

the Red Sox when I was young, but the real explorations
were of family, not sports, memories. I saw my father and
our relationship differently from the way I had before
the first draft unrolled.

A few paragraphs down I found myself writing: ▪

My father was always at the store, off to New York on business
or at Tremont Temple for morning and evening services, for
Wednesday-night prayer meeting, and for church business
meetings in between. He left home before breakfast and came
home late. My uncles were more father to me than this quiet,
mustached man with thick glasses and a sad smile.

■ And later I saw our childhood relationship, as complicated as most such relationships, in a way I had not seen
it before: ▪

I knew then, in some strangely reversed way, that I was my
father's instructor in childhood. He was the oldest son of Scots
who indentured themselves to Fall River mills to get to America,
and I could never get him to remember a single childhood game.

Stern economic facts and equally harsh Calvinist beliefs
made life a serious business. He had wanted to be a teacher or a
minister, but his father, who was to die young and pass his paternal responsibilities on to his eldest son, took my father out of
school on the morning of his fourteenth birthday in 1904, the
moment he could be removed legally from the classroom.

I taught my father to toss a baseball, but he always tossed it
like a girl, in a day when girls threw baseballs like a girl. Father
never got the hang of a football and on each two-week summer
vacation in Maine I tried to teach him to swim and failed.

■ And as I came to the end of the draft, I saw how
through all the conflict and pain of my leaving his
church and his political party—even while I deserted
his ambitions for me and lived a writer's, even an academic, life he could not understand—we had one sure
line of communication that was always open. ▪

Now looking back, twenty-one seasons after his death, I realize
that when we could not talk politics or religion, when he could

not understand the dreams of a writer and the world of a reporter turned professor, we could talk baseball. It was the one certain world we shared.

That first day at Fenway opened lines of communication that lasted all our days together. He talked the Red Sox to me when he came late from a trip to New York and found me sick again, and he could not talk of the fear he must have felt for his only child. And I talked the Red Sox to him the time when it was my duty to say "cancer," when we had to discuss his failing heart and the time for finally letting go.

Similar discoveries take place when the writing is less personal. I have ghostwritten corporate annual reports, written for Cabinet officers, written memos as an administrator, news stories as a police reporter, academic articles and textbooks, and the fun of each writing task comes for me in writing what I did not expect to write. I didn't write what I had already thought, but I thought by writing.

Suggestion

Try experiencing discovery through writing by following these suggestions:

1. Think of a person, a place, an event that is important to you. (If you can't, don't worry, brainstorm by listing the specifics that come into your head for three to five minutes, then circle the one that surprises you the most and start writing or draw lines between the specifics that connect and explore that territory in writing.)

2. Write as fast as you can for five minutes. Do *not* worry about saying something silly; do *not* worry about spelling, penmanship, punctuation, grammar. Just write. Concern with these matters is important but it comes later; now is the time for creating the map, not making it neat and presentable.

You will produce a text that surprises you. That is the central experience of the writer; we expect to write about

Fenway Park and find out that we are writing about our fathers. That is the joy of writing and the importance of writing.

The Explorer's Attitude

The explorer has expectations but seeks the unexpected: the animal with two tails, the mountain range that is not on any map, what hides beyond Mars. Most people fear surprise, but the writer-explorer must become comfortable with surprise, the sentence that turns on the writer and attacks his or her strongest belief, the phrase that undercuts the argument, the word that drags the essay writer toward an unpredicted conclusion. This is what thinking is like: strapping on skis and careening down on an unfamiliar mountain slope. Writing carries you forward at top speed and sometimes you crash, but it is worth it when you have a thought new to you, when you understand your world in a way that you never have before. Then writing, like skiing, becomes addictive, a need to write what you do not expect to write.

This Is a Draft

To allow exploration, the writer has to understand that a draft is being written. The word *draft* is the same as an experiment in science. It is not a final thing, but an act of seeking that may very well fail. But the failing will be instructive.

A draft may fail in meaning. It may not make sense but it will show how sense may be made. A draft may be confused but reveal the need for order and indicate the way meaning may be constructed. The language in the draft may be awkward and unclear but reveal in a few words or a line how the voice of the text may be tuned so it becomes clear.

Hope for Surprise

Normally we are taught to look for error, to correct mistakes, to make everything right—the way the reader expects it to be. The time does come for dealing with the traditions of form and language, with the expectations of the reader, and that is the main business of this book, but the time is not now.

Good writing often lies in the unexpected line, not the expected. John Fowles counsels, "Follow the accident, fear the fixed plan—that is the rule." The accident—the wrong word that is exactly the right word—is the place where an effective piece of writing often takes off. Writers look for the edge, the place where there is new information, a different angle of vision, a form pushed to its limits, a voice that has not been heard before.

I Can't Write Better than I Can Write

Follow Bill Stafford's odd-sounding but profound advice. His counsel has helped me more than any lecture on composition I ever received, and I copy it in the calendar book that is always at my side:

> I believe that the so-called 'writing block' is a product of some kind of disproportion between your standards and your performance. . . . One should lower his standards until there is no felt threshold to go over in writing. It's *easy* to write. You just shouldn't have standards that inhibit you from writing.
>
> I can imagine a person beginning to feel he's not able to write up to that standard he imagines the world has set for him. But to me that's surrealistic. The only standard I can rationally have is the standard I'm meeting right now. . . . You should be more willing to forgive yourself. It doesn't make any difference if you are good or bad today. The *assessment* of the product is something that happens *after* you've done it.

Yesterday, for example. I had a long, frustrating day working with writers at the *Boston Globe*. I got up at 4:40 A.M., drove in a wind/rain storm through Boston traffic, spent a long day, suffered traffic jams on the way home, ate a late dinner, stayed up watching the Boston Bruins on TV, slept badly, got up late, tired and grumpy, had disturbing phone calls, and did not want to meet you on this page this morning. Most of all, the task seemed impossible. The deadline is closer each day and the mountain I have to climb, the draft that is being dramatically rewritten, seems larger each day. I need to do more; I need to do it better. I can't do more; I can't do it better. And so I give you Bill Stafford's advice and listen to it myself. All I can do is write what I can as well as I can. I have to forgive myself.

We have to develop the courage to write *not* as we wish we could, but as we can. And I use the term *courage* purposefully. I was in the paratroops in combat but I am often scared by the blank page. It is like a night jump into nothingness. If we are to learn to high jump, we must lower the bar until we can get over it; if we are to learn to write, we must lower our standards until we can complete a draft. Each day I face impossible standards as I come to my desk; each day I must learn to accept the writing I can get done. First I must draft; later I can revise and improve.

Suggestion

Take the piece you have written for the previous suggestion or something you have written before. Read it through quickly, then turn it over and write it again. Take only five minutes to write this new version; write so fast that you push your knowledge of the subject and your feelings about it beyond your expectations of what you had to say. Don't be afraid to contradict what you have written— or thought—before. You are thinking by writing.

What Am I Looking for?

Beginning a new writing project, the inexperienced writer panics: How can I plan the writing when I don't yet know what I'm going to say? The writer can't plan what will be said, but the experienced writer knows how to plan the expedition into the unknown so that something worth saying will be discovered.

A Topic on Which I Can Become an Authority

The word *author* has a direct connection with authority. When writers publish, *they* are the authority. Effective student writing occurs when the student finds a way to take an assignment and move it to his or her own territory, writing with authority.

The assignment might be on ethics and the student might write from experience—and from internal conflict—in faking a football injury or taking a cheap shot, in reporting or not reporting what you find in a child's room when baby sitting or what you saw your boss do with the money in the cash register after work. The possibility of becoming an authority varies greatly with the assignment but when there is free choice the student writer should choose to explore a territory in which the student may become through reflection, research, and writing, an authority.

A Topic with a Productive Tension

One of the great mysteries of our peculiar trade of writing is why so many writing topics that seem promising don't work— and why some that don't seem promising to the editor or teacher work for a specific writer. This has puzzled me in my own work, in my students' writing, in the writing of the professionals I have counseled as writing coach. In the last year or so I think I have finally discovered the reason: tension.

The writing that we enjoy reading and remember usually explores a productive tension—a conflict that is clarified and often resolved, at least temporarily, by the end of the draft.

Animal experimentation is not a topic; why we must sacrifice monkeys in animal research and why we should not torture monkeys for medical science are productive topics. Adoption is not a productive topic. There is no tension. I wish I were adopted, the search for my birth mother, I'm glad I was adopted, why no one would adopt me, and how the law exploits foster children may be productive topics for a particular writer.

A few of the forms of productive tension include:

- Between forces within the text: those who attack and defend animal experimentation.
- Between reader's expectation and what is actually said: The reader expects that animals are used in the search for a cancer cure and finds that many are sacrificed in the hunt for a new pancake makeup.
- Between the writer and the subject: The writer expects to be horrified visiting an animal lab and finds that the monkeys are treated with care and respect.

There are many sources of tension in every topic. List them to see which ones may be productive. And as you move through the process of revision, realize the importance of tension. Tension provides the energy that drives the reader through the text. It is a significant element as you revise for meaning, audience, order, evidence, voice. Look for the productive tension within the evolving draft and make it work to clarify your meaning—and keep your reader moving down the page.

A Topic on Which I Can Focus

Most explorers limit their explorations; Henry Hudson didn't attempt to explore the entire continent in front of him but, instead, a single river in a place that would eventually be called New York. The river is now called Hudson. The explorer doesn't go into space but to the moon—or a specific orbit.

The best discoveries are made when the explorer has a focus. The topic for the writer should be limited to something that can be achieved during the time allowed; for example, a weekly assignment is different from a semester one. Not the judicial system in the United States but in one county in Oklahoma; not all the cases in the courts in that county but one case; not all aspects of that case but the single issue—tension or conflict—that illuminates the judicial problem the writer is exploring.

And yes, the explorer will make discoveries that expand or contract the original focus. The case in the court may not reveal a judicial problem by one in law enforcement or the insurance industry, but the problem was found because of the focused expedition into this area.

A Topic That Will Instruct Me

Most important for me is that the topic has a fascination for me or a need. I am fascinated with the process of revision, first explored it in writing twenty years ago. Now I want to return and discover both what I have learned about revision in those two decades and what I can learn now, so I write this book. I am surprised that at age 65 I need to understand my complex relationship with my father, now dead 21 years, but I do and I accepted the Fenway Park assignment mentioned at the beginning of the chapter because I knew I would learn something about my father and myself, and I need to do that.

> ### Suggestion
>
> 1. Brainstorm topics that you may want to explore. Take only five minutes; work fast and be willing to be silly. When you are done, circle anything that surprises you, draw arrows between any that connect.
> 2. Take a topic you have had to write on and brainstorm to see what other ways you might have been able to respond to the assignment.

How Do I Explore in Writing?

Most people think of language as something we use *after* we have thought, but writers use language to think. Words are one of the best tools for thinking. Words reveal what we know and go beyond that in connecting what we know in new ways so that we discover we know more than we thought; words capture research, reading, observation, and allow us to connect it with what we know so that we can develop new understandings. Writing is thinking.

Develop a Critical Eye

Writers question and that alone often makes society uncomfortable with writers. One of the first acts a totalitarian regime does is to control—silence—its writers; one of the first signs of the end of a totalitarian regime is that writers are asking questions in public.

Writers work in the territory of doubt. They are skeptical. This does not mean disbelief or cynicism; that is the belief there can be no belief. Writers are optimists, realistic optimists; writers are builders, makers of meaning. But to make their meanings they stand apart.

The writer is often the person observing the party from the hall or while in the center of the party rising above it in a trick of the mind, seeing what everyone, including the writer, is doing, and discovering by observation and reflection what it means.

It sounds lonely, but I have found that it is not. I think more of us play this game than admit it. We learn from our detachment that human ability is an essential talent, for it allows us to comprehend what is happening to us while it is happening as well as afterward. The detachment is not cold or cruel but should be compassionate; it is the essential quality of humor that makes us see the distance between what should be and what is.

To explore the world in which we live, we need to develop a critical eye that witnesses what others do—and what we do as well—so that it can all be studied, understood, and shared.

Look for a Pattern

The writer brings order to chaos. The world confuses; the writer clarifies. Where others see a jumble of unrelated events, facts, details, ideas, experiences, the writer sees a pattern that reveals meaning.

Look for these patterns. The pattern may take the form of a theory that underlies and unites all the elements, a narrative in which everything is ordered by chronology, a sequence of actions and reactions or problems that are solved but give birth to new problems.

There are many forms of patterns, but once you glimpse a pattern, you may find everything fitting into it, and you will have some writing to do. The draft tests the pattern and the final draft shares it.

Seek a Revealing Specific

The pattern may be discovered as you fly over life and observe it from afar, and a previous pattern may be imposed upon life to explain it. What doesn't fit is amputated or bent so that it will fit in the appropriate box.

The best patterns, ironically, do not come from distance but from within the confusion itself. The economist and writer John Kenneth Galbraith has said:

I would want to tell my students of a point strongly pressed, if my memory serves, by Shaw. He once said that as he grew older, he became less and less interested in theory, more and more interested in information. The temptation in writing is just reversed. Nothing is so hard to come by as a new and interesting fact. Nothing so easy on the feet as a generalization.

Eudora Welty says, "What discoveries I've made in the course of writing stories all begin with the particular, never the general." It is the fact that usually gives rise to the best patterns. I call such facts *revealing details.* They are specifics that resonate, that give off potential meaning the way a piece of phosphorescent wood glows in the dark. These meanings are often personal, private until we explore them and find the developed meaning we can share with another person.

The fact that my father had no childhood was such a detail for me. It was merely family history until I put it in a historical context of immigrant grandparents and their children at the turn of the century and my father in the Depression years before the five-day week and then the pattern I revealed in my article had a special resonance for readers of my age.

Catch an Image

An image, a quick snapshot in the mind, will often lead a writer to a territory that needs exploration. When I saw my first dead enemy in combat I saw a belt buckle that said, in German, that God was on *his* side. My ministers had assured me God was on *our* side. It started me thinking—and writing—about the role of religion in war.

Find a Problem

Humans are problem-solving animals. We are never as happy as when we find a problem that we believe we can solve. I remember the excitement the surgeon tried to suppress when he suggested taking out my heart and working on it. He had a problem to solve—and I certainly hoped he could solve it. He did.

Writers often see a territory to explore when they spot a problem that is central to the material and that interests them. Some of the most common problems are:

- What does this material mean?
- What caused this material to develop?
- What will happen because of this material?
- How will this affect people?
- How do I show readers they need to know what I have to say?
- How can I make this material clear to the reader?
- How can I make the reader think about this?
- How can I make the reader care?

These are just a few of the many problems that can provide a starting place for the writer.

Ask a Question

A good piece of writing is a dialogue between writer and reader and it may help the writer see the territory to explore by anticipating the reader's questions:

- Just how dangerous is it?
- Why hasn't somebody done something before?
- What can be done now?
- How much will it cost?

These questions can be asked of many areas from pollution to health care to the preservation of books in the library.

Listen for a Line

The starting point for my explorations is in the fragment of language I call *the line*. I had been dependent on the line for years but did not realize it until I began to write a column, "Over Sixty," for the *Boston Globe*. The frequency of the assignments and the ease with which I fulfilled them interested me. I examine my own writing methods to see what has worked when the writing has gone well—the best way to teach yourself to write—and realize there was a moment when I knew I had a topic to explore through writing.

And then I realized that the same thing happened when I wrote a chapter for my novel, a chapter of a textbook, a personal letter of sympathy, a memo, a poem, an article, or prepared a talk. Each time was marked by the arrival of a line.

What Is the Line?
It is a fragment of language that contains the tension that will
release the energy to propel the draft forward.

What Do I Mean by Tension?
Many topics, subjects, or ideas for a piece of writing are without
the necessary tension. I have written this before, but it so important I must repeat it here. We attempt to write The Causes
of World War II, Symbolism in the Poetry of Marianne Moore,
The Death of My Grandmother, or the infamous My Summer
Vacation. They may be important territorial claims that stake
out a place where writing may take place, but they are not yet
pieces of writing waiting to be written.

The draft begins for me when I have a conflict to resolve,
an experiment to attempt, a question that needs answering, a
territory that demands exploration, a problem that needs solving. These do not come to me in the abstract but in language.
They are not general but specific, concrete, active, demanding
to be written.

There have been cases where a single line has sparked
writing for me:

- "I had an ordinary war" was a line in my daybook that made
  me start the novel I am writing. What becomes ordinary in
  war is truly terrifying.
- "What happens when a writer teaches writing?" The answer
  became my first book on teaching writing: *A Writer Teaches
  Writing.*
- One day as I was crossing the street, a bee that must have
  been riding on my beard suddenly flew away. It seemed as if
  it had flown from my mouth and I remembered the same
  surprise when I spoke in school. I was shy and the teachers
  and I agreed on one thing: I was not doing well in school.
  That feeling led, a few days later, to this poem:

  Back Row, Sixth Grade

  It is always October.
  I trudge to school,
  kick a stone, leap the crack
  that goes to China,
  take my seat in the back row, jam

my knees under the desk,
avoiding chewing gum, waiting
for recess. The substitute
teacher hesitates
by the door. The bell
rings. She commands
attention to the text.
I cannot find my place.
There is no meaning
in the words. Nearsighted,
I squint at the blackboard:
the tails of dogs, a banana,
a winding river, a diving
hawk. I am in the wrong grade,
in a foreign school, another
century. I stare out the window,
learn how a robin drives a squirrel
from her nest, imagine
a fear of wings. Teacher
calls my name. I speak,
as surprised as if a bee
flew from my mouth.

- I heard myself say after visiting a late-middle-aged man with a young wife, "I'm glad I have an old wife," and that led to an article.

My life is full of lines—I visited Guilford College, a Quaker school dedicated to pacifism and conscientious objection, to find their football team called the Fighting Quakers and thought of the violence of some demonstrating pacifists and wondered if . . . . Writing corporate reports, accurate crime reports as a military policeman, many different forms of writing, I find the line helps me spot the territory to explore through writing.

We have to remember that the line is a secret code through which writers speak to themselves. The full meaning of the line will only be realized by the writing. It is a way for the writer to mark a territory, to stake out a claim that may be mined successfully or not. Everyone else looking at that line, those hard-scrabble acres, sees what is ordinary, but the writer sees what may be hidden below the surface.

How Do I Encourage a Line?

Encourage is the right word. You cannot force the line. It is the product of mental play, conscious and subconscious thought that is deceptively casual. My lines come to me before the writing desk. Sometimes, faced with a deadline, I will brainstorm fragments of language, hoping to stumble across a line. Most lines, however, arrive when least expected, when I am driving, shopping, talking to other people, reading, watching TV, taking my morning walk, sitting in the car waiting for my wife, sitting in a restaurant waiting for my luncheon companion. I am never without pen and paper, cards stuck in my pocket or my daybook—a journal or log I keep with me—and I scribble down every line that floats by in the stream of consciousness in which we record and comment on the life we are living.

What Does a Line Look Like?

The line does not appear in one form but many:

- *A word.* One word may contain an essay, a poem, a book. A single word may carry in it a whole world of meaning for the writer that can only become clear to the writer and, later, to a reader when the writing is done. It may represent an event, an idea, a person, a place that is packed with potential meaning. The single word *Lee* may mean many things to many people but it has special meaning to me, for it is the name of my daughter who died at twenty, and that single word appears on my daybook pages again and again, each time having the possibility of becoming a piece I must write.
- *A phrase.* Two or three words may hold among them the material for pages of writing. Those words are often in conflict or a state of tension with each other. Abortion foes who call themselves pro-life imply their opponents are pro-death. Body count was a term used during the Vietnam War to obscure the fact that Americans were killing and dying. We have a living will— the strange term for a document that authorizes our family to withhold life support systems and give us the gift of death. I

could play with any of these terms and produce an essay that would reflect my views on abortion, war, or euthanasia.

- *A fragment or sentence.* The lines blur between phrase and sentence but often I see—or hear in my head—a fragment of language—a line—more than a phrase but not as complete as a sentence—that gives off glittering potential. Other times the line arrives as a complete sentence. I once wrote an editorial that came from the line "I cheered when they dropped the atomic bomb." I explained how we who had just finished fighting in Europe felt when we were scheduled to go directly to the Pacific and fight on the Japanese mainland. My opinion today might be different, but to understand the decision, we have to go back to the time when the decision was made.

There is no one form for the line. It is only a private grouping of words that inspires you to write.

What Does a Line Sound Like?

Voice is the magic in writing. It is the background music that anticipates and supports the meaning and more. It is the element that makes the reader trust the writer. It is the force that makes the reader read on. It is the quality that allows an individual reader to hear the individual writer on the page.

The experienced writer hears the voice of the draft in the line. I often hear the voice of the text—my voice tuned to the subject and the audience—in the line. To put it another way, the line tells me if I am detached or involved; if I am angry, sad, nostalgic, in a humorous mood; if I want to argue, persuade, document, record, entertain. We all have many voices: a home voice, a school voice, a dorm voice, a locker-room voice, a visiting-grandmother-in-the-nursing-home voice, a courting voice, a done-courting voice, a Saturday-night voice, a job voice, an officer-I-didn't-know-I-was-going-too-fast voice. Hundreds of voices and we can hear, in a single line, the voice that may be appropriate for the draft to come.

What Do I Do with the Line?

Follow it. Write as fast as you can to see where the line will lead you. Joan Didion says:

Nota bene:
   It tells you.
   You don't tell it.

In effective writing of a first draft, the writing is in charge, the material tells you how to write it.

Suggestion

Sit back and think about a territory you may explore in writing. Don't think hard: Drift, daydream, float over the territory with your mind's eye. Then take one of the techniques in this section—or more than one—and apply it to the one you are investigating through writing. Try, for example, to list revealing specifics, record important images, draft lines.

Where Do I Explore?

In your head. The writer's workshop is a portable, bone-surrounded chamber called a skull that contains all the writer knows. Experience and research, formal and informal, continuously restocks the writer's workshop with new information that usually affects what is already in inventory.

In the World

One of the delights of the writer's life is that the writer is allowed—even forced—to learn about what interests the writer. The writer has the obligation to explore the sources that may illuminate the subject. Writers use *research* as a verb—they research what they are writing by using all forms of the library, increasing their awareness, and interviewing authorities.

Libraries

Immerse yourself in information about your subject. Information is power, information establishes authority, information is the resource from which you can draw to produce effective writing.

Libraries, government agencies, and professional organizations are filled with books, magazines and journals, newspapers, articles, reports, academic papers that will give you the concrete information from which you can construct your draft. There are computer banks of information that will also deliver important information to the writer. Take advantage of all these sources to keep restocking your brain with new information.

Observation
Writers collect an inventory of information with which to write by engaging all their senses in gathering important fragments of information. We see, we hear, we smell, we taste, we touch.

Interview
Seek out people who are authorities on your topic, those who are affected by your subject. It is flattering to be interviewed. Don't be shy. Most will want to talk, and they will arm you with important information.

Memory
Writers have a special form of memory—and so do you. Few writers have a quiz-show memory for unrelated facts. I certainly don't, but when I write of important events in my life that happened when I was a child, in combat, at college, the parent of small children, the specific, revealing information I need appears on the page. As I revise, more and more details appear, first the shape of the room, later the patterns in wallpaper, rug, and lace curtain, who was in the room, how they dressed, what they said, the smell of my grandmother's afternoon handkerchief. I remember what I didn't know I knew.

Suggestion

Try it: Write a page, as fast as possible, about an important event or place in your childhood. See how much you remember. Quickly write it again, see how much more you have stored in your writer's memory.

In Imagination

Imagination is not something apart from what we know but an extension of it. Robert Cormier speaks of the magic question that ignites imagination:

> What if? What if? My mind raced, and my emotions kept pace at the sidelines, the way it always happens when a story idea arrives, like a small explosion of thought and feeling. What if? What if an incident like that in the park had been crucial to a relationship between father and daughter? What would make it crucial? Well, what if the father, say, was divorced from the child's mother and the incident happened during one of his visiting days? And what if . . . .

Ask: What if? Look into the material to see where the lines of perspective will take you, where the narrative line of the story or article will extend, what new problems will arise from the solution being used to an old problem, what changes will take place intended and unintended, how individuals will be affected.

Within the Assignment

The assignment itself gives an opportunity for exploration. Copy the assignment down if it is given orally or mark it up if it is passed out on a sheet of paper. Make sure you understand the assignment. Ask questions to make certain you know what is expected. Then step back and brainstorm the different ways the assignment might be completed; circle the assignment, studying it from different angles. When you see a territory—a way of responding to the assignment that interests you—try it.

Suggestion
Take an event from your life or an assignment from a class and use the techniques described in this section—memory, for example, or the library to discover how you can explore your topic in that way.

How Do I Start Exploring?

There are two principal ways of exploring through writing and I use both of them. One involves plunging right in and the other standing back and creating a plan. At the moment, I plunge in on poetry and fiction, half plunge in and half plan my newspaper columns, carefully plan my academic articles and textbooks. A great deal depends on the writing task itself, the personality of the writer, and the experience of the writer with the form being used—it is hard to plan for a voyage you've never taken. And when you just plunge, you may find the need to stop and plan; when you plan, you may find the need to abandon the plan and just plunge in.

The Discovery Draft

An inefficient but wonderful way to begin writing is to create a discovery draft in which you put aside your notes and write to discover what you have to say and how it may be said. The writing may "loop around" to use Peter Elbow's term, but it will keep coming back to the itch that needs to be scratched, and it will do it in such a way that the form and structure of a piece of writing will come clear. In the writing it becomes an argument, an essay, a narrative, an analysis.

There are some conditions that produce the most effective discovery drafts.

Welcome Surprise

Put aside what others have written and any preconceptions about what you expect to write. Be open to the subject and yourself. You are thinking, not writing what is already thunk. Your opinions may twist, turn, bend, and change. You may see connections that contradict, doubt, question, illuminate, confuse, clarify, obscure. Invite surprise, invite learning, invite thought. Write what you do not expect to write.

Velocity

A discovery draft must be written fast; only by speed will you outrun the censor and cause the accidents of insight and language that produce effective writing. F. Scott Fitzgerald said, "All good

writing is swimming under water and holding your breath."
William Faulkner used a different metaphor to communicate a
similar idea, "There are some kinds of writing that you have to do
very fast, like riding a bicycle on a tightrope."

Length

The discovery draft should take you further than you have any
idea that you can go. It is important to use up the material you
know before you write and start writing what you don't know
you know. To do that, you should not write one paragraph or
page but many. Five pages is better than one, ten better than
five, twenty better than ten.

Silence the Critic

Do not worry about spelling, punctuation, grammar, organization; just let language flow. You are just creating a sketch, not
painting the ceiling of the Sistine Chapel. You are looking for a
rough draft, really a predraft of what you may explore in a
more carefully written, even a planned draft, later.

The Writing Plan

The writing plan can be helpful *if it is not taken too seriously.*
Remember it is a sketch, not a contract. No one will sue you if
you don't follow it. In fact, the purpose of the plan is to cause
thought, and thinking will usually limit, change, or contradict
the plan. What I am writing at the moment does not follow my
careful plan and that delights me. But I do not regret the plan
or the time I spent creating it; it is because of the plan that I got
here.

Draft Titles

The poet John Hollander says, "I feel the title is a very small
aperture into a larger area, a keyhole perhaps, or some way of
getting into the poem . . . ." Each draft of a title is a predraft
of the entire piece of writing. Remember that a title is not a
label but a few words that catch the essential tension in a topic
and, often, the writer's point of view toward it.

Here is a label:

Experiments on Animals

Here are some titles:

Are Lab Monkeys Dying for Your Lip Gloss?
Animal Sacrifice Saves Human Lives
When Is Cruelty to Animals Justified?
A Visit to an Animal Experiment Laboratory
A Visit to an Animal Torture Chamber
Will Human Experiments Be Next?
What the Nazis Did in the Name of Science
I Live Because Lab Animals Died
The Last Days of Charley Chimp

The list could go on. It only took a few minutes to write that list, but see how each one points the writer toward a different piece of writing, different in the research required, the documentation collected and used, different in language, form, structure.

Drafting titles for ten minutes or twenty—or in fragments of time—can save the writer many false starts and even complete drafts that have to be tossed aside when the writer discovers the territory to be explored.

Draft Openings

Joan Didion says:

> What's so hard about the first sentence is that you're stuck with it. Everything else is going to flow out of that sentence. And by the time you've laid down the first *two* sentences, your options are all gone.

And that's the reason I like to play with opening lines that are similar to titles. The opening line is similar to the title in that it allows the writer to try a number of different approaches in a short period of time. Each opening line does many things. It establishes:

- The subject and limits it
- The central tension within the subject
- The meaning the author will communicate
- The author's point of view toward the subject
- The form of the piece of writing
- Its pace
- Its length
- The documentation necessary

- The reader to whom it is addressed
- The voice in which the text speaks

All of these issues may be established in a few lines that can be drafted and revised in a few minutes, while writing each draft might take days. As a former paratrooper, I have written several essays on the holidays that celebrate militarism. Notice, as I draft some openings, how much is decided by those few lines.

> Tomorrow the nation will celebrate war. I will not attend.

> On this holiday I used to hear the bands play Sousa, watch the flags dance in the sunlight, admire the precise lines of marching men, worry that I would miss my war. I didn't. There were no bands, no flags, and most of the marching men died.

> "They want you to be in the parade, Don."
> "Not me. I was in the official victory parade for World War II, right down Fifth Avenue in New York City."
> "That must have been exciting."
> "It was one of the worst days of my life."

> The family thinks I spend Memorial Day alone. I do not parade and I sit by myself at the far edge of picnics. But I am never alone. I sit with the ghosts of men who remain forever young.

> On this holiday I am always surprised. I never expected to come home from my war.

In effect, I have written five drafts and I might write dozens more before I wrote the first draft. The time would not be wasted. When I began to write I would feel sure about the direction I was taking and many of the opening lines I abandoned would return through the piece.

Draft Endings

Many writers know the ending in the beginning, some even write the ending first. I rarely do that but I often have an idea of what I will say in the ending and if I am planning my writing, I make a note of it.

It helps to have a sense of destination—we're going to the mall, to the lake, to the cabin—but, of course, we may not get there, we stop at McDonald's, run into some friends, hang out downtown but we would not have gone into that McDonald's if we hadn't been heading for the lake. We need the same sense of destination in planning to write but we also need to be able to go somewhere else if that is where the writing takes us.

Sketch a Trail

If you know the beginning and the end you can make notes of the landmarks that you will pass on the way. You may be able to sketch the three, four, or five main points you want to make to draw your reader through the writing.

Again, remember this is not the rigid plan of the formal outline, it is a sketch. And it is not a contract that must be followed; it will change and it should.

The Reader's Questions

Another way to start exploring is to ask the questions the reader will ask. In most cases you can anticipate the reader's questions—usually about five—and the order in which they will be asked. Then you can answer the questions. There are no set questions. They come from the area you intend to explore.

Here are the questions I might anticipate if I were going to write a piece about SATs, a pet hate of mine.

- What are the SATs?
- What do they not test?
- What do they test?
- How important are SATs?
- How can they be beaten?
- How are students limited by SAT scores?

I'd jiggle them into a better order, an order that would draw the reader in and prompt the reader to ask the questions in this order.

- How important are SATs?
- What are SATs?
- What do they test?
- What do they not test?
- How are students limited by SAT scores?

I can see writing that article now. It is not *the* order in which it should be written. It is only *one* way it might be written. I'd also take out the following question since it is a whole article in itself: How can they be beaten?

This is an easy, logical, and effective way to create a rough "draft" or vision of a piece you may write.

> ### Suggestion
>
> Try one of the techniques above or one of your own design to make a sketch of the way you might use language to explore a territory.

How Do I Keep Exploring?

Here are some tips that will make it easy for you to keep exploring your world with your language.

Nulla Dies Sine Linea

Never a day without a line. Horace, Pliny, Trollope, Updike, and many others. Writers write. If I know I am going to write, my mind consciously and unconsciously prepares, turning over a compost of ideas and lines as I walk, eat, watch television, visit, shop, read, drive, meet, sleep. That isn't inspiration. It is preparation. Paul Valery talked of "the inspiration of the writing desk." That is where the writing arrives. Make writing a daily habit so that it becomes an easy and natural part of your life.

I go to my writing desk by habit with as much enthusiasm as the mechanic to the garage, the checker to the supermarket, the student to the class, but then, when I am in language, writing what I do not yet want to write, something happens and I am led by words I do not expect to meanings I had not foreseen. The writing inspires me—and it will inspire you.

Use Fragments of Time

The time at the writing desk can be short—in fact it doesn't need to be at your desk. You can write during breaks at work, in the car, waiting for someone to pick you up, between classes. As a full-time writer, I try to write—and that's writing, not staring out the window, planning, editing—two hours a day. But I used to put on a parking-meter timer and write fifteen minutes the first thing in the morning. Write a hundred words a day, two hundred, three hundred. Write a page a day and you'll have a 365-page draft of a book at the end of the year. I started working a half-hour a day on a novel. I missed a few days and many days I only get a quarter of an hour in but it starts to add up. Today I finished the tenth chapter and have 108 pages of draft finished.

Stop When You're Ahead

Hemingway and Faulkner would stop writing in the middle of the sentence when they were interrupted or at the end of the day so they could immediately start writing.

Complete the Expedition

Push on, get to the end. If you are stuck, mark the text with "fact TK" for information to come, leave a blank of a few spaces or enclose it in brackets, [   ], to signal a place to which you must return. Write badly if you have to but finish so that you can visualize the entire draft and see what needs to be done when you revise. The imagined draft is never as helpful as the real one, no matter how full of holes and how sloppy it is.

Suggestion

Write a draft that is worthy of reading and revising. How do you do that? Follow the counsel in the chapter. Use some of the techniques in the chapter to find a territory to explore and a way of exploring it. Then write fast, pushing the edges of what you know so that you produce a rough draft that has the potential to say something important after it is reread and rewritten. Follow Annie Dillard's counsel: "One of the few things I know about writing is this: spend it all, shoot it, play it, lose it, all, right away, every time. Do not hoard what seems good for a later place in the book, or for another book; give it, give it all, give it now."

3

Read to Discover

Just before I start to read a first draft I feel a secret excitement, yes, and a touch of fear. I will discover I had nothing to say.

But then when I read, I discover I have too much to say. I go from despair to panic. How will I deal with all the material that lies in the draft? The answer is that I won't. I will focus on a single meaning and develop that; but first, to know what that meaning should be, I have to read to discover the full potential of my draft.

Reading as a Reader

I have to distance myself from the text. This isn't easy. A draft is personal. It is my voice, it contains the essence of what I am in the same way that my face reveals me. Some of you may like mirrors. I don't. I feel young, even sleek, dark, lean, sexy, and my mirror destroys the illusion. I have never recovered from the person who came into the city room and asked for that "moon-faced reporter." He meant me! I have grown a beard that has gone from reddish brown to gray to white, tried to keep up-to-date in spectacle style, but my hair, now white, is thin and the lines in my face reveal wear—not wisdom. I can't rewrite my face.

But I can rewrite my drafts, so I have more courage in confronting what I have written than I have in facing my morning mirror. I try to read my words with a stranger's eye. I want to judge my draft against the reader's needs, not my expectations. You, my readers, crowd around my desk chair, peer over my shoulders at my computer monitor as I read. I hear every in-drawn breath and yawn, friendly chuckle and not-so-friendly giggle, see your pointing fingers, hear and feel your doubt, disagreement, distrust. If I let you in my study when I wrote, I would never write. I write alone but now there is no escape. Come on in. I must read with you readers.

Role Play a Reader

If I cannot achieve enough distance to avoid a paternal defensiveness about my child-text, I role play a reader. I choose someone I know who is intelligent but doesn't know—or care—about my subject. I walk around my study the way that person walks, talk to the empty room the way that person talks, sit in my chair the way that reader would sit, and read my draft as that person would read it.

I try to visit my text as a stranger, hearing what it actually says, all the messages given off by the words themselves and all the messages given off by the climate of the words. We know when we visit somebody that we receive messages from what the person says, but we also get messages from behavior, from the way the room is arranged, what is in it, all the elements that communicate; supporting, qualifying, or contradicting what our host says. It is just the same in writing. A text creates a world, and the direct message of the text is supported, qualified, or contradicted by the world of writing in which the message has been placed. It is that world that often tells us to trust—or not to trust—the writer's text.

When I role play, I try to get the feel of my text and the environment in which my text exists.

Fastreading

We have talked about the benefits of fastwriting, and there are benefits to fastreading as well. My first reading is always at top speed, the way the reader will read. Flying over the surface of my draft, I am able to overlook my inevitable typos, misspellings, unchecked facts and quotations, strange grammatical constructions, off-target words, illogical structures. Those problems will be dealt with later. Now I read for one meaning.

Reading for Discovery

It hasn't been easy but I have trained myself not to take my first draft into the back room, bring out the rubber hose, and give my draft the third degree. I used to attack my text, trying to beat it into shape, making it suffer all my unproductive feelings of failure, hopelessness, ignorance, and guilt. Not anymore. I read with anticipation, in good humor, knowing that the text will surprise me—and teach me what it means. I ask of my draft:

- What does it say?
- Do I mean what it says?
- How can I make that meaning clear?

As I read, I try not to mark the text or fix any problems. I may make a few notes in the text in bracketed, indented, boldfaced, or underlined text on my word processor or I mark up the typed text, scribbling in the margins and drawing on the text itself, but I do not line-by-line edit. It is too soon for that, and if I become involved in the details I will miss the priority problem of finding a meaning I can develop and clarify with revision.

The many meanings may be obvious. They may even include what I expected, but in the best writing the meanings are usually changed, qualified, sharpened by the writing of the draft. The meanings within the most successful first drafts are entirely different from what I expected or, when I am fortunate, contradict my most basic assumptions. Writing is thinking, not merely a record of previous thinking.

Reading Fragments

Often potential meanings are hidden in a word, a phrase, a line. I have had to teach myself to read fragments, and so should you. When we read our drafts we are like the archeologist who finds a fragment of a bowl, the preserved ashes of a fire, a sharpened piece of stone, and then uses a trained imagination to create a civilization.

There are many forms of fragments that reveal meaning. Here are some that I frequently discover.

Code Word

These are words that have a private meaning for us. In my case these words include *right tackle,* the football position I played; *paratroops,* the service I served in during World War II; *oboe,* the instrument played by our daughter who died. There are hundreds of code words in our language, many of them less personal than those I described above, but they are words that radiate personal connotation. I read *basement,* an ordinary word, and suddenly remember that was the word in first grade that took on a new meaning and a terrifying, seductive mystery—when I went to first grade the basement was where you were sent when you raised your hand and said, "I have to go," and it was where other little boys told you . . . . I probably won't write an essay on the word *basement,* but I could. It is there, waiting to be written, hidden in that single word, *basement.* I can see that place, smell it (unfortunately), start to remember what I heard there, saw there, feel the excitement and the shame. All in one ordinary word.

Revealing Detail

When I had my heart bypass, I was part of a machine for ninety-one minutes. That we can survive while surgeons diddle around with such a vital organ as the heart opens the door to the poems and columns I have written about that experience. It could lead, in my hands, to a novel; in another writer's hands to a screen play, a nonfiction book on heart surgery, to a play, to a biography of a surgeon or an autobiography of the patient. A stimulating fact may be revealing detail. I am told that we graduate more lawyers each year than Japan has in total. Now there is a way to talk about our sue-happy society and the dismal swamp of our overworked judicial system in which justice delayed so often means injustice.

Significant Phrase

In New England, we all look forward to Indian summer, those days in the late fall when the weather suddenly turns warm. But it was a phrase born in fear. In colonial times the pioneer farmers worked their fields with muskets nearby and huddled at night in crowded forts where they could protect their families against attack by Indians. When it started to get cold, the Indians would not attack and the families could live in their homes beside their fields. Then the weather would change and the Indians would return, surprising individual families. *Indian summer* has for me two hidden meanings, meanings that have a tension filled with possibility for writing.

Haunting Image

After we buried my father, I went into my parents' bedroom and found my mother sitting alone on the edge of their double bed that had been worn to the shape of their double forms. I am haunted by that image and we all have those snapshots of memory that carry enormous loads of meaning that we may choose to explore and share by writing.

Think about what you notice, what sparks an emotion in you, what you think about when you are alone, and you will begin to see the meanings hidden in fragments within your first drafts.

Reading Other Clues to Meaning

There are many elements other than fragments that reveal meaning to the writer. Some of the most significant to me include the following.

Music

Writing is heard. Writing is speech written down, and the text is heard, more than seen, by the writer. The melody of the text often tells me where the meaning is and what it is. I hear my own words telling me that an event has more significance than I realized, and this evolving meaning makes me angry, sad, happy, amused, instructed. The music of the text makes me pay attention, and in paying attention I find new possible meanings.

Pattern
Scanning a draft, I see a pattern of possible meaning emerge. Information gathers in clusters, divides along an unexpected fault line, engages in civil war with other information. I see in the draft a direction, a pointing toward meaning.

Thread
When I read a draft fast, I often begin to see a thread woven through the text that I was not aware of while writing. Images, phrases, metaphors, echoing details and words, lead me toward a meaning I did not expect, but am compelled to pursue. I am taught what to write and how to write it by the thread that runs through the draft.

Reading What Isn't Written

It is most important to learn to read what isn't written—yet. We know day because of night, the pain of hate because of the comfort of love, loneliness because of companionship, and the reverse of all those may be equally important. What *is* reveals what *isn't*.

I have often started to write of death and discovered, in the draft, that I should celebrate life. This morning I woke from dark dreams, aware of my mortality, but that awareness, as I took my morning walk, made me celebrate the cool winter sun rising through the branches of the trees. I had special appreciation for the mist rising off Mill Pond and delighted in the gossip of the ducks, the raucous cries of the sea gulls, the silent dignity of the swans.

What isn't on the page can tell you what should be on the page, what territory you should explore with writing. The holes in the draft, the subjects you have avoided, the gaps you didn't see, the evidence not yet presented, the conclusion not yet drawn, may all reveal the meaning that demands pursuit.

The Dialogue with the Draft

The clues to meaning come in my response to reading the draft, what I hear myself saying in the privacy of my skull. I talk to myself as I read my first draft, and this dialogue helps me see the meaning I need to develop and share in the text. Here are some examples of what I hear myself saying that may reveal meaning:

- "Mary Ellen needs to know this. She would be interested."
- "What does this mean? I've never thought of this in this way before."
- "Hey, what about that? Maybe I'll find out something if I write a draft focusing on that."
- "This is new stuff; well, at least I've never written about it."
- "Whoa. This is not what I thought I said."
- "I do not believe *that*. It's just the opposite of what I believe."
- "Clumsy writing here. I wonder why I'm having so much trouble saying that."
- "I like that. Not bad, Murray. That business there really works."
- "This idea (word, phrase, fact, tone) keeps popping up. It seems to thread its way through the whole draft."
- "You again? This one thing seems to dominate everything else."
- "Ah, now there's an interesting tension between . . . ."

Suggestion

Take one of the techniques I've introduced in this section and use it to mine your draft for potential meanings. If that doesn't work, don't worry. Take another one and try it.

What Works?

Most writing instruction by teachers—and editors—is error oriented. Everyone looks to find out what is wrong. But effective writing is built from what is right, not wrong.

I don't even like those words *right* and *wrong*. They seem too clear, too absolute, and writing isn't like that. Everything in writing is relative. Rarely is it a matter of right or wrong, traditional or nontraditional, formal or informal, correct or incorrect. Writing takes place in a complex context of subject, reader, form, and language. That is why writers use different terms:

- What works?
- What needs work?

Nonwriting English teachers sometimes hate those terms and I can understand why. Standards, traditions, styles, formalities have the appearance of academic certainty; they can be applied to many pieces of writing. And it is true that all of us write within traditions, we all have a history and a context. Traditions are in every act of composing, but in evaluating the draft the writer works from within the individual work.

What works implies an organic standard, what is right for this meaning, what will help the meaning come clear for a reader. In reading for revision, writers do not look first at external standards but internal ones.

And they go further. They look first at what is successful, not what has failed. Recently, in a newsletter I do as writing coach for reporters at the *Boston Globe* I wrote:

> 'I'd like to improve my writing but I don't know what to do. I write OK and I get in the paper but I think I could write better.'

> 'Decide what are your strong points—voice, interesting angle of vision, revealing details, organization, making complex issues clear, getting people on the page to come alive, humor—and push them.'

> 'Shouldn't I work on my weaknesses, what I do wrong?'

> 'Sure. If you call the Mayor of Boston O'Brien, write in a complicated-sort-of-like-you-know-confused-tangle-of-syntax, shape up. Strive for competence, but if you want to break out of the pack, go with your strengths and make them stronger.'

> 'Who says?'

> 'I say and so do other writers. Go to the edge, develop you strengths, push them, exaggerate them. Art is selection and exaggeration.'

'But what I think are my strengths, editors often think are my weaknesses.'

'Nobody said it would be easy. Listen to Fay Weldon:

> What others say are your faults, your weaknesses, may if carried to extremes be your virtues, your strengths. *I* don't like too many adjectives or adverbs—I say if a noun or a verb is worth describing, do it properly, take a sentence to do it. There's no hurry. Don't say 'the quick brown fox jumped over the lazy dog.' Say, 'it was at this moment that the fox jumped over the dog. The fox was brown as the hazelnuts in the tree hedgerows, and quick as the small stream that ran beside, and the dog too lazy to so much as turn his head.' Or something. Writing is more than just the making of a series of comprehensible statements: it is the gathering in of connotations; the harvesting of them, like blackberries in a good season, ripe and heavy, snatched from among the thorns of logic.
>
> Having thus discouraged the apprentice writer from overuse of adjectives, I turn at once to Iris Murdoch and find she will use eighteen of them in a row. It works. What is weakness in small quantities, is style in overdose. So be wary of anyone who tries to teach you to write. Do it yourself. Stand alone. You will never be better than your own judgment, and you will never be satisfied with what you do. Ambition will, and should, always outstrip achievement.'

'That seems risky?'

'Sure is. You have to learn to deliver the expected story in the expected way to be an effective member of the Globe staff and you also have to save something of yourself, to develop your own potential in your own way if you want to be one of the best writers on the Globe.'

'A balancing act.'

'Always. Creativity is the child of the uncomfortable, conflict-filled marriage between freedom and discipline.'

The student has the same challenge as the *Globe* writer; the student has to satisfy the teacher's expectations and also develop that which is most individualistic within himself or herself as the writer.

Effective writing is built from finding the strengths of a draft and extending them. Of course there are elements that need to be eliminated, developed, changed, but the primary building materials come from what has potential. To find what works, I read for potential.

Meaning

I read potential meanings, experiments in thought that deserve to be attempted; a fleeting idea that needs to be pursued, captured, and developed; a question that I need to answer; an answer that deserves a question; an evaluation or opinion that needs to be made; a trend or theory that readers need to know.

Form

In reading, I sense narratives that need to be developed; hear poems; spot essays; catch the hint of significant arguments; see lab reports or book reviews, analysis or interpretations that need to be made.

Structure

Patterns arise from the text. It is almost as if I look through a special microscope and see, beneath the type, a pattern that needs to be brought out, examined, and shared. Other times I see lines that run across the pages, circling and connecting facts, words, lines. These are architect's sketches; each study will show how an essay may be shaped, a term paper ordered, an argument declared and answered.

Information

Specific information—descriptive details, revealing statistics, significant quotations—often exude potential meaning. A word, a fragment, a line may give off a meaning that can illuminate an entire text.

Voice

I read aloud, listening to my draft. The music of a draft, perhaps more than any single element, tells me what I may choose to develop from the first draft. I have taught myself to hear the potential in fragments of language that communicate meaning or feeling.

It's wonderful if two or three elements in a draft "work" but one is enough. Some of the elements that may be successful include:

- Voice
- Information
- Order
- Form
- Meaning

Rarely do any of these elements work consistently in a first draft. I may hear the voice in an occasional paragraph or sentence, sometimes only in a line, a phrase, a word. That is enough. I seek fragments—that's all—that can be expanded and developed through revision.

As we read our first drafts we need to concentrate on what works and what may work, to see those subjects and those qualities in our writing that we need to cultivate.

Suggestion

Stop. Sit back. Think of a piece of writing that you have done well. That has never happened? Sorry. Think of the one thing in a piece of writing that has been the least bad. What is this one quality—the subject you chose, the angle of vision you took toward it, the way you organized the piece, the manner in which you reached readers and sparked a response in them, the humor you communicated—or anger, the line or two that really made your meaning clear? Look at what you did that was successful and write down some suggestions on how you can develop and extend that quality in the writing you will do in the future.

What Needs Work?

The main rule of a writer is never to pity your manuscript. If you see something is no good, throw it away and begin again. A lot of writers have failed because they have too much pity. They have already worked so much, they cannot just throw it away. But I say that the wastepaper basket is a writer's best friend. My wastepaper basket is on a steady diet.

That's the advice of the wise old writer Isaac Bashevis Singer, and we should pay attention to it. What a relief it is to throw away. The first draft should be cluttered with possibility but once the meaning is found, the writer can toss out what isn't needed. When the clutter is carted away, the writer can concentrate on what supports and develops the dominant meaning of the draft.

What Goes into the Wastebasket

The inexperienced writer falls in love with each collected fact, each written phrase; the experienced writer knows it is essential to research and write with abundance because only in an excess of material is significance found, but that it is just as important to heave most of that abundance into the trash once the meaning is found. This is not a failure of excess. All that stuff was necessary, but now it needs to be cleared away so the writer can concentrate on revising the draft.

Some of the items that you will see piled on the sidewalk in front of the writer's house are:

- *Potential leads:* sketches of ways the final draft may open *and* leads that might have to be followed to document the final draft.
- *Revealing specifics:* details that illuminate the great variety of potential meanings that lie within a productive first draft. Those that reveal the meaning selected remain; the rest are tossed.
- *Interesting lines:* fragments of language that contain the many tensions within the subject, each giving off possible voices, meanings, trails through the material.
- *Answers without questions, questions without answers:* essential to the search for meaning, but now that meaning is found most can be tossed away so the writer will deal with the few essential ones left.
- *Resonating images:* pictures in memory or imagination that may lead to meaning in the writing of a first draft or communicate the meaning to a reader. Those that are important now must be saved, the others eliminated.

- *Ideas:* theories, clues, hints, hunches that were necessary to finding a meaning but can be eliminated now if they do not relate to the discovered meaning of the draft.

What relief, even joy, there is in getting rid of all that gets in the way of developing the chosen meaning that is to be made clear and complete by the process of revision. All that confusing inventory of notes and failed drafts was valuable, but now it can be discarded so that the writer can concentrate on what is left.

What Needs Support and Development

When the writer has gotten rid of all that clutter it is possible to stand back and consider, in an orderly fashion, what needs work. Now a sequence can be imposed that makes the rest of the revision orderly and achievable. There is a priority of revision once the meaning is selected that will control the final draft.

Experienced writers may deal with this hierarchy of revision problems simultaneously or jump back and forth between them, but there is a logical, efficient order that can be followed in which the problem solved establishes a foundation for the solving of the next problem.

Meaning

An effective piece of writing says one thing. There is a dominant message and everything in the piece leads to that meaning or develops from it; every element in the final draft advances the writer's principal meaning.

Audience

The revising writer needs to estimate what the reader knows of the subject and what the reader needs to know. The writer must be able to ask and answer the reader's questions when they are asked.

Order

The form and structure—the order within the form—must reflect and communicate the meaning of the piece. An argument has an expected form that must be developed or worked against in a clear and constructive way if the reader is to be persuaded.

Evidence

Readers are hungry for information that communicates and documents each point. This information must be accurate and authoritative, interesting and convincing to make the reader believe the writer's meaning.

Voice

The language of the text—its music—must speak clearly to the reader. Each paragraph, sentence, phrase, word must do its job.

This sequence that develops and communicates the meaning of the text will be dealt with in detail in the next chapters of the book.

The Draft Instructs

Recently I had the opportunity to spend a weekend with a jazz trio who improvised. I was a few feet away and I could hear what they said to each other before, during, and after they played; I could see *and* hear how they listened to the music, each in his own way, exploring the music hidden within a familiar melody. They knew the various jazz traditions—dixieland, Chicago, K.C., swing, be-bop, fusion—and the nonjazz traditions—rock and roll, country, classical, bossa nova, new wave—but their most productive explorations occurred when they worked within the music, listening and learning from what they heard.

I have the same experience every day at my writing desk. I get drawn away, remembering what I was taught by teachers and editors, what I read, what is traditional in my craft and in the form in which I am writing—all that is important to absorb and adapt to the writing task—but the most valuable instruction comes from the writing itself, from the draft that is evolving under my eye and in my ear.

The writer knows that the answers to most writing problems lie within the draft. If you read the draft carefully with an open mind, the draft will reveal its potential meanings and the ways those meanings might be developed.

In the next chapter we will discuss in detail techniques to choose a dominant meaning and focus on it; but for now, revel in the potential of the draft. Before the draft you—and I— wondered if we had anything to say and the bank account read zero; now we have too much to say and our problem is finding focus. The bank account is loaded and we have to decide how to invest our wealth.

Suggestion

Go back and scan your draft, listing each potential meaning. Then consider each meaning and note the ways it might be developed, argument and perhaps persuasive personal essay or scholarly analysis for this one; an autobiographical piece or narrative for another meaning; a research paper for a third meaning. By writing down each meaning and sketching how each might be explored and communicated, you will realize the inventory of writing material you have on hand and the inventory of solutions you have to the problems of each writing task.

4

Revise for Meaning

When the ambulance screams up to an accident the paramedics have to decide which patient is most seriously injured and then they have to decide what is that victim's most serious problem. There may be cuts and bruises, broken bones, external and internal bleeding, difficulty in breathing. The medics have to decide immediately which problem threatens life and what can be done about it.

When I read first drafts from students, from professional writers I coach, from my own computer, the priority, draft-threatening problem is focus.

I may see a draft that is sloppily prepared, full of mis-spellings (and if this poor speller can catch them, the writer is in *real* trouble), punctuation problems, incorrect facts, illogical structure, and an uneven, awkward style, but I have to probe for the real problem. It is, most likely, a lack of focus.

The writer may have found the meaning, but now it needs to be focused on the central issue within that meaning. The meaning may be "drunk driving kills." Sadly that is both true and common enough, but now we need a focus on a particular cause such as peer pressure to be macho or a prevention program that works; such as a car that sniffs alcohol on your breath and refuses to start. If there is no focus, the lack breeds all sorts of other problems.

Often, I see a slick, polished piece of writing that just doesn't add up. The typing is beautiful, the manner clever with well-turned phrases; there are no errors of fact or grammar, but I don't know what it all means. My editor recently suggested I reread one of my columns. It fitted this category. The underlying problem? Focus.

Another frequent problem is the carefully wrought draft that is totally without surprise. It is dull, tedious, predictable, boring. Nothing is wrong but, yawn, who cares? I know what the draft will say before it says it. The problem may be premature focus. Either a teacher or editor gave the writer a rigid assignment that prohibited discovery, commitment, and thought by the writer, or the writer lazily grabbed hold of the first focus that the writer thought of and jammed the subject into it regardless of the fit.

Say One Thing

One of the biggest differences between the successful writer and the unsuccessful one is the successful writer says one thing. One idea dominates.

The writer may have known that single idea before writing, it may have become clear to the writer during the writing, or the idea may have been discovered through the reading of the draft. But once the idea is recognized, it has to be developed and clarified by revision.

How Can I Find That One Thing?

Look for the point of tension at which the forces in the topic collide.

Questions To Reveal the Focus
Sometimes it is a good idea to back off, turn the draft over, or store it so it is not on the screen and think about the subject. After writing and reading the piece:

- What surprised you?
- What did you expect to read? How was what you read different from your expectations?
- What do you remember most vividly?
- What did you learn from the writing and the reading?
- What one thing does a reader need to know?
- What is the single most important detail, quote, fact, idea in the draft?
- What do you itch to explore through revision?
- What single message *may* the final draft deliver?

Sharpen the Focus
Once you have an answer to one of these questions, then you can sharpen it. Some rules for sharpening the focus:

- Use as few words as possible.
- Play with specifics from both sides of the issue that is in tension, avoid generalizations and abstractions.
- Use nouns and verbs, especially active verbs.
- Reveal the central tension.

Titles and First Lines
The focused meaning may, in fact, become the title. When I was free-lancing magazine articles I would start writing an article by brainstorming a hundred or more possible titles in fragments of time as the research was winding down. Each title was a window into the draft I might write.

The fragments of language that focus meaning often become the first lines of a piece of writing. As a journalist, I am a great believer in writing the lead—the first line, first paragraph or three, the first page—first. The entire piece of writing should grow out of the beginning and the lead can establish:

- The question in the reader's mind to be answered in the draft
- The direction of the draft
- The pace of the writing
- The form
- The voice

But What about All the Other Good Stuff?
There are two kinds of good stuff. One can be used to support and advance the focus of the story, clarify and communicate your

meaning, and the other is material that will draw the reader's mind from your message.

Supporting Material

Kurt Vonnegut, the novelist, once said, "Don't put anything in a story that does not reveal character or advance the action." That's a good rule for nonfiction from corporate memo to literary essay.

Every piece of information, every literary device, every line and every word must support, develop, and communicate the meaning. Each comma, verb, statistic, reference, descriptive detail, transition, summary sentence should relate in a direct way to the central tension of what is being written.

All these team players must work toward a common communication goal. Revision is the process of selecting and shaping who plays on the team so that each plays its role effectively in the final draft.

The texture of the final draft, its quality, comes from the variety of all the material that supports and communicates the message. My son-in-law, Michael Starobin, is an orchestrator on Broadway. The composer of the musical comedy establishes the melody but it is the selection of violins, clarinets, trumpets, drums, and synthesizers that communicates the melodies in all their color, supports the action on the stage, and makes a major contribution to how you think and feel in the audience.

The melody by itself is hardly enough and the meaning, focused and sharpened, needs all the supporting material to reveal its full significance and make the reader react emotionally and intellectually.

Distracting Material

One of my editors at *Time* used to say that you could tell a good story by how much good stuff—quotes, facts, anecdotes, draft paragraphs—you threw away. Effective writing grows from abundance.

The material you have collected through research and the thinking you have done through writing that must be cut from the draft is not wasted. It is all money in the bank. You may not spend it on this draft, but it is there, to be drawn on in the future.

And in a way it is still in the draft even after it has been cut. The marble that has been cut away from the statue made an essential contribution to the statue. It is there in the revealing.

All that you know and do not include in the draft is sensed by the reader in the same way that we are impressed by the power held in reserve by the great singer or athlete. It underlies and supports what the singer or athlete performs.

Suggestion

When starting a book, John Steinbeck used to write on one side of a single three-by-five card the potential meaning of the draft. He would change it as he wrote and refined the meaning but it gave him a sense of destination. That is a valuable revision device. Try it. Read your first draft and then write in *one sentence* the meaning you have discovered that you want to develop and communicate through revision. Put it at the top of the draft you are going to revise.

Frame Your Meaning

I can remember my simple box camera and the wonder of my uncle's complicated, expensive Kodak with its expanding bellows. In high school I saved up for months to buy an Argus— I think it cost twenty-five dollars—the first inexpensive camera that used 35-millimeter film. Now I could take candids, shots that were not posed with the subjects holding their breath.

Many children today have their own cameras and families have a whole range of cameras, including ones that can make television movies with color and sound. Grandma wouldn't have believed it.

We are film literate even if we are not readers. When I write my novels I film them in my mind. It is natural with we who watch television, go to movies, and make our own films. And, in a sense, I do the same thing when writing nonfiction.

You may be learning about writing, but I bet you know how to frame a picture in focusing it. It helps us to realize how much we know about writing without knowing we know it. Writing and rewriting go better when we can face our tasks with confidence, and most of us feel confidence in taking pictures these days.

What to Leave Out

Draw a frame around the subject. You can even do this physically by scanning the draft and drawing a line through everything that has to go. Sometimes I circle the material and mark it with an arrow heading off the page—or a question mark. Most times the decision is easy, but sometimes I have to scan the draft a number of times to see if it should go or remain. The test is simple: Remember Kurt Vonnegut's advice and save what advances your meaning. Everything else must go.

What to Keep In

Keep in what moves your meaning forward. The remaining material must develop and communicate the focused meaning. You might complain, "But almost everything went. My draft has shrunk!"

Good. This is an important stage in the writing process. When we have found our focus it gives us space for complete development. Maybe half the material can be saved or only a third, or a quarter, a page? Now you have the room for the material you will add during the revision process.

Revision for the published writer is often a far more radical process than the inexperienced writer imagines. The master writer knows that what is taken out is necessary to get the draft to the place where it can be made to work. The writing cut isn't a sign of failure but progress toward an effective final draft.

Most of us write a first draft that skims over the surface of our topic. That's appropriate. We are searching for our focus, our meaning. Once we find it, then a lot of the material we included can be jettisoned. Over the side with it. No regrets.

> ### Suggestion
>
> Make a sketch—of course you can draw well enough for that—of what the reader should see when reading your draft. You may want to make a floor plan that will show where the camera is, what it can show, and what it cannot. Can you do this with an idea? Of course, then it is a diagram that shows what is included—and excluded—in an essay on the French Revolution, in a plan for a new product due in a marketing course, in a report on environmental waste.

Set the Distance

An important issue in focus that is rarely discussed in most textbooks is the matter of distance. We can stand nose to nose with our subject or back off and see it from a mountain top, a space shuttle, or even—by writing from a historical perspective—from a distance of hundreds of years.

The focus, as in a camera, depends on how far away you—and the reader—stand from the subject. The distance cannot be set by a rule book but depends on the subject, your purpose in writing about it, and the reader.

When To Use Close-ups

Close-ups bring immediacy. We do not photograph the field of spring flowers but move in on one poppy, show the whole blossom, or go even closer to a petal, perhaps catching a bee stopping by for breakfast.

In the close-up we don't look at the entire government but the legislature, not the House of Representatives and the Senate but the Senate, not the committee structure but a committee, not the committee but a single senator, not the career of the senator but one revealing vote.

We can, with the close-up, expose the details of a scene, a law, a scientific experiment, a crime, a vote. We can reveal complexity and simplicity, cause and effect, action and reaction. But we may not understand what it means and so . . . .

When to Step Back

We step back to put the flower, the vote, in context. We show the fields of wildflowers that stretch for miles to the Rockies, we show the historical and theological roots of the abortion issue and the pressures that caused the senator to take a position and now reverse it.

The distance shot allows us to make the generalization from the documentation, to put the anecdote, the quotation, the statistic, the scientific discovery in perspective. We can show what came before and predict what will follow. We provide a context. But what if I need to do both?

When to Zoom

You have a zoom lens. Use it. Don't just stand in one spot and try to see what's going on from there. Take your reader in close for emphasis, for clarity, for dramatic effect to make the reader think and feel, then zoom back so the reader understands the full implications of what he or she has been shown.

Don't move forward and back wildly, without purpose like Uncle Max with his new video camera at the wedding. Move in close smoothly, draw back halfway, close in once more, then back away again in a pattern that serves the reader, giving the reader the information and the experience needed to become involved in your subject.

Suggestion

Take that sketch, floor plan, or diagram you did before and move the camera farther back or in close or concentrate the diagram or make it even more distant to see how that one element can change the impact of the text.

The Importance of Focus

Drafting is including, but revision is the craft of selection. Revising a draft takes hundreds of executive selections. Each word may affect the meaning of the word next to it and words a page away; each line has implications for other lines; each sentence and paragraph changes the emphasis, pace, impact of other sentences and paragraphs; each piece of information influences the value of other pieces of information.

How do you make these decisions? By using focus. Every decision is resolved by its value to developing and communicating your focused meaning.

Suggestion

Select one specific in a piece of writing you plan to do. Focus on that specific and list what must be included in the final draft if you make that specific central; change to another specific and see what on your previous list isn't necessary, and then list the new specifics that now become necessary.

5

Revise for Audience

We write for ourselves—and others. We write to learn—and to share what we have learned. We write to record, celebrate, complain, entertain, persuade, and for many other reasons; but the act of writing is not complete until we are read.

To communicate effectively, to attract and hold readers, to convince readers, we have to be able to stand back from our drafts and read them with a stranger's eye. This isn't easy.

A few of us look in the mirror and see beauty no matter that the nose twists to the left, the eyes are too small, the chipmunk cheeks are filled with nuts. Most of us look in the mirror and see ugly. We appear to have three eyes, great rotting tusks, and volcano skin. Neither view is how we are seen by others. Most of us are not beautiful but attractive, not ugly but interesting.

We have to be able to stand back and look at our draft with the eyes and ears of the reader if we are to make the changes that—most of the time—make a text appeal to readers.

Identify Your Reader

When we talk, most of the time we speak to an individual. We adapt what we say and how we say it to the other conversationalist, reading the responses, verbal and nonverbal. We hear words and inflection, emphasis, pace, rhythm; we read the conversationalist's gestures, facial expressions, nods of agreement or disagreement.

Experienced writers are aware of their readers in the same way; they imagine a reader nodding, smiling, growling, stopping to puzzle out that last sentence.

Write to Yourself

Writers do this, first of all, by writing to themselves. Edward Albee says, "I write for me." Toni Cade Bambara adds, "First and foremost I write for myself." Graham Greene concludes, "My only readership is me."

Writers talk about writing for themselves but students know *they* are writing for a teacher. And I know—because I am a writer—that writers are writing for editors and, ultimately, readers. But I also answer the question, "Who do you write for?" by saying, "For myself," knowing that Michael Rosenberg, my editor, is right now standing just over there on the other side of my computer screen.

Well, what's this all about? I think writers mean two important things when they say they write for themselves:

1. Writers are their own audience in the sense that they are similar to their readers. They do not "write down" to their audience. It doesn't work. Effective writers write *across* to their audience. They think and feel the way their readers feel; they do not stand apart but beside their readers. They write for themselves.
2. Writers know they have to be themselves. They have no choice. Writing reveals. I was an editorial writer for three years but I was never asked to write an editorial that expressed an opinion opposite to my own. The publisher knew it wouldn't work, my insincerity would show. If you try to be someone you cannot be, you will be exposed. The

writer has to work within all the limitations of the craft— the requirements of subject, audience, form, purpose; the limitations of length and genre. Within those limitations writers have to be true to themselves, meet their own standards, produce products that are theirs.

The student writer and the professional writer are not that far apart. Both have to work within the practical limitations of time, space, knowledge, tradition, editor/teacher/reader expectation and yet still manage to be themselves. And to monitor themselves during and after writing they have to be— simultaneously—both writer and reader.

Writers stay in tune with themselves while writing and reading what they have written. They write to themselves and talk back to the writer saying such things as, "Hey, slow down, you're getting too far ahead of me"; "This is good, I could take a bit more of that"; "You've lost me"; "I simply don't believe you"; or, "That's great. Do more of that."

Write to *One* Other Reader

After yourself, it is time to read from the point of view of a single reader.

If I am writing to a particular person—the widow of a friend who has just died, a college official who might give me a grant, my editor—then, of course, I read from the point of view of that individual. If I am writing for a general or unknown audience, I choose someone I know, a person who is intelligent, but who doesn't know—or care—about my subject. I role play that person. I may even speak like that individual, walk around my desk the way that person walks, then read my draft fast as a reader will do.

I have written for magazines that sell to millions of readers but you can't write to a million readers. Writing and reading are private acts, one on one, and I have to imagine one person reading my draft.

Re-create Your Reader's World

Each of us brings a whole world to the reading of a text. I just read a wonderful—and terrible—book, *Warfare—Understanding and Behavior in the Second World War* by Paul Fussell (New York: Oxford University Press, 1989). That was my and the author's war. I brought to it many shared memories and many different ones. He was an officer, I was a private; he was infantry, I was a paratrooper; he was wounded, I was not. When we read a book we create, in a sense, a private book between ourselves and the author as we read each line with our similar and different experiences.

My wife had a very important job as the secretary to the scientific adviser to the Secretary of War in the Pentagon. When she reads Fussell, she will read a different book. When my daughters, who were born long after the war and raised during the Vietnam era, read it, they will each read a still different text.

One of the great challenges of the writer is to produce a text that will cause readers to draw on their different experiences and still understand what we have to say. The first step is to recognize that our world may be different from the reader's.

We have all had teachers who, when asked a question about what they have already explained, simply repeat the explanation. They live entirely in their own world. The explanation fits their knowledge and their way of thinking, so they cannot understand why their explanation doesn't make the topic clear to every student. The master teacher understands the enormous diversity among students, delights in it, and makes what is being taught clear in many ways or in a way that can be grasped by students with very different backgrounds.

Recognize the Other Worlds of Readers

Be aware of the worlds of knowledge and belief your readers may inhabit. I am writing a novel that, in part, involves World War II. I must remember that my readers may not know what an M-1— our rifle—was, or a C-47—the two-engine troop-carrier plane from which we jumped. They may never have heard of the Maginot Line, the string of fortresses that were to have protected France, or the SS, the special Nazi political-military force; may not even know of the Holocaust that attempted to eliminate all Jews, or know that Russia and China were on our side, Germany and Japan on the other.

We must recognize that our readers may not share our religion; our political party; our economic perspective; our faith in education; our respect for haggis, the national dish of Scotland, which is basically a sheep's stomach filled with porridge, and which is a heritage from the English conquerors and absentee landlords who took the most edible parts of the sheep back to their kitchens in England.

The Vital Skill of Empathy

To understand where my readers come from when they say "ick" to the haggis or hold their hands over their ears—or pull at their noses—at the stirring drone of the bagpipes, I must practice the rare skill of empathy.

Empathy should not be rare, but it is. Empathy is the ability to put yourself in the skin and the heart and the brain of people who are different from you. Writers can imagine the thoughts and feelings of readers when they read the draft.

To develop the skill of empathy, an ability that will serve you well in any career you choose—and in your relationships with those close to you—you make yourself hear from the point of view of a person who does not live under the assumptions of the person who is speaking.

Hear someone going on and on against abortions and think how the listener, who has had one, feels; hear about plans to fly to Bermuda for spring break from the point of someone who may have to drop out of college for a semester to make money for tuition and books; listen to a patronizing remark about the way blacks can really jive from the point of view of a black who has little sense of rhythm and is interested in particle physics or Mozart.

Just about the most important thing that happens in college for most of us is that we realize that there is not one world—our parent's world—but many worlds, contradictory and gloriously diverse. When we know of those worlds, we can write from our world in such a way that the inhabitants of other worlds will read our texts in their own terms. We will communicate.

Give Evidence Your Reader Will Believe

To persuade, we must document our writing with evidence that is accurate, appropriate to our message, and persuasive to our readers. What authorities do our readers respect, what form of evidence—anecdotes, academic footnote or reference, scientific example—will make them believe?

Our reader may be persuaded by an anecdote but put off by a statistic—or just the reverse; a reader may believe the person quoted is an authority or a buffoon; a reader may be flattered by a legal term in Latin or feel put down and resentful. Empathy allows us, most of the time, to recognize the difference. Sexist language, which I have learned to avoid, is language that insults or excludes the majority sex. How do I know what language is sexist? I read from the point of view of a woman and cut out any language that indicates there is one sex (male); that, by pronoun reference implies that, for example, all writers are male; that excludes, insults, puts down, makes fun of women. I know what these are by reading from the point of view of a woman. And if I am in doubt, I show my draft to a feminist friend.

Speak Your Reader's Language

We have enormous experience and control over our language before we get to first grade. We know how to speak to the grown-ups who raise us (I started to write *mother* and *father*, then, through empathy, realized that some student readers might not have a father or a mother, or might even have lost both, and changed the sentence between the time it left my mind and arrived on the screen), to playmates, to neighbors, to strangers, to teachers.

This ability to speak in terms appropriate to our listeners increases with maturity and experience. When I was English Department chairperson we arrived at our decisions through long, wandering, rhetorical discussions but the dean was a social scientist who loved statistics. I translated our decisions into numbers for him.

Suggestion

Turn yourself into someone you know and respect but who doesn't care about the subject of your draft. Scan your draft and write a brief review of your piece *from that reader's point of view.* Note what that reader likes and dislikes, believes, and questions.

Ask Your Reader's Questions

The effective writer carries on a conversation, in print, with the unseen reader. This isn't magic, but the trained ability to imagine the responses of the reader to the subject and the text.

Anticipate the Reader's Five Questions

Or four or six or seven or three. A few key questions, that's all the reader really asks. They are the simple but significant and obvious questions that can't be ignored.

Ask for a job and the employer asks what is your experience, who are your references, what are your work habits, why do you want this job, what can you do for me? We can anticipate those questions asked out loud or silently and prepare ourselves to answer them. It is the same way with writing. We can anticipate the five significant questions the reader will ask.

Order the Questions

Once we know the questions, we can anticipate the order in which the reader will ask them, and this is a great help in organizing a draft. That dean I wrote to always asked, "What's it cost?" I could anticipate the question *and when he would ask it* as he read my memo. I could not avoid it, but I could read his mind and give my answer in terms that made my case as strong as possible.

I have found it helpful to brainstorm the questions first, and then put them in the order the reader will ask them. I've tried, with my students, to ask and order the questions simultaneously, but then we usually missed questions or did not happen on them as well as when we listed the questions and then ordered them.

Answer Them

Once you know the questions and where they will be asked, answer them. You can't hide, not when you are a writer. The questions, especially the ones you do not want to answer, will be asked. If you don't know the answer, then you'd best let the reader know you don't know the answer.

Suggestion

Write down the five—or four or seven—questions the reader will ask while reading your draft. Put them in the order the reader will ask them. Answer them.

Use Test Readers

Use test readers—friends, teachers, editors—to help you see what works and what needs work, *but be careful.* Most people read entirely from their own world. They read the text they expect, the text they hope they would have written, the text that makes them feel comfortable.

Doris Lessing reminds us, "You have to remember that nobody ever wants a new writer. You have to create your own demand." As writers we have to walk the line between creating something new that will be rejected by many readers at first and writing strictly within the traditions that will communicate to many readers. If we get too far ahead of our potential readers, we will have no readers; if we stay too far back in the pack of tradition, readers will find nothing special about us and turn to other writers.

Writing for Bad Readers

We have to be able to write for unsympathetic readers, readers who do not like what we have to say or how we say it. We cannot afford to write only for those who agree with us and admire our writing style. We must face enemy readers.

Usually this is done in a class writing group; unfortunately it may be provided by a teacher or an editor, and if the structure doesn't provide it we may have to seek enemy readers to discover if we are communicating to those we want to reach.

I have three personal rules for responding to enemy readers:

1. I pay attention to their outrageous responses, the crazy comments I never expect. Most of them turn out to be crazy, but if a test reader thinks that I am being anti-semitic, as one reader of a novel did when I thought I was being pro-semitic, then I had better pay attention. Other Jewish test readers said I was sympathetic and accurate, but I needed to know that.
2. I pay attention to those comments that make me realize I've been caught trying to get away with something. Perhaps I'm trying to cover a gap in logic with a clever phrase or write myself over a crevasse in my evidence. I snap to and fix those weaknesses.
3. I pay attention to those comments, no matter how mad they make me—and they do—that reveal this reader didn't understand what I was saying. It's my job to go more than halfway when writing, and I usually come up with alternative ways of saying the same thing that answers the reader's complaints.

But I do not depend on enemy readers. I learn the most from friendly readers who support me but make suggestions that cause me to write better.

How to Find a Good Test Reader

The best test readers for me are those who can read my intent and help me write better in my own way. Most readers place a formula over what I write and then suggest how I can satisfy their formula. My most valued readers have the unusual ability to read with my voice, from my own angle of vision. They can be tough, demanding, critical readers but they do it within my context. They express respect for what I am trying to say and how I am trying to say it, and they suggest ways in which I might strengthen my draft.

I have a test for readers. If I want to write when I leave our conference, then I know I've found a good reader for me. Their comments may be critical, the problems they have exposed may cause extensive rewriting, but when I leave them I am thinking about new ways of writing the next draft, and I am itching to get to the word processor. Those are the readers I treasure.

Tell the Reader What You Need

To make sure my test readers serve me well, I tell them the kind of reading I need. Here are some of the comments I hear myself making:

- "This is an early draft. I just want a quick reading to see if you think I'm on the track of something."
- "Chip, can I try this lead out on you? Do you think it works?"
- "This has a long way to go, but will you scan it and see if you think I've got it lined up right?"
- "Mekeel, do you think there are any lines worth saving in this poem?"
- "This voice is different from what I expected. Do you think it's right for this article?"
- "Evelynne, I don't know if this works at all. Let me know if you think we should toss it."

And at the end of the drafting process, I give it to my wife. "Okay, it's done, I think. Give it a close read. Does it make any sense, where do the commas go, typos, the whole ballgame?"

The test reader will be able to help you most when the reader knows your opinion of the draft, where you—the writer—think you are in the process, what you see as the draft's strengths and weaknesses.

Responding to Criticism

We all have a natural defense against criticism: We don't like it. And that is good, but we have to work to develop a constructive attitude so that we can make use of criticism, rejecting what isn't relevant, making use of what is. For years—decades?—I overreacted to criticism, resisting all of it and believing all of it; I swung between rage and despair. Neither was helpful. I think I made progress when I realized that there is no absolute right or wrong in writing. There are a hundred ways to be wrong in an essay—and a hundred ways to be right. It is a matter of choice, what works and does not work for you, on this subject, in this form, for this reader.

I used to feel that there were absolute standards for writers. If I passed it was like the bar exam, and I would be a writer. If I flunked I'd have to go into business and get rich. But writers are self-appointed. All it takes is a private declaration and a supply of postage stamps. The critics are as fallible as my drafts. It is up to me to accept and reject each criticism as I think it relates to the draft under my hand.

Responding to Praise

Praise can be more dangerous than criticism but I need it. I do not only need praise for psychological reasons, probably relating to my toilet training; I need praise because, as mentioned earlier, writing improves more from the extension of what works than from the correction of what doesn't work. And I am never sure of what works.

It is usually easy for me to spot failure. In fact, I often err on the side of spotting failure that isn't failure. I despair easily when I read my drafts; the reality rarely matches the dream. I need readers who reassure me, tell me what works for them, how, and why. Then I can build on that.

Creating Your Own Writing Community

Writing is a lonely craft and I need a community of writers with whom I can share shoptalk, grump and groan, gossip and network, share writing in progress.

I've established my writing community in several ways. When I meet someone—or hear of someone—interested in writing, I try to meet that person. Often that means inviting the writer to lunch or telling him or her that I'd like to get together and talk about writing.

If we seem compatible, I share a draft. If my reader's response sounds honest, intelligent (knowing in a writerly way), and *if it makes me want to write* I elect this writer-reader to my club by sharing other drafts. Usually he or she begins to share drafts with me, and we share writing on writing as well as conversations about writers we are reading and how our writing is going.

Some of the members of my writing community are my editors, but most are writers, young and old, experienced and inexperienced, who share the terrors and satisfactions of our craft. I have a list in my calendar book to whom I send most drafts and even daybook notes. I look at my list and see that it includes one sixth-grader and a high school graduate who hasn't yet gone to college. There are professors and graduate students, two editors, journalists, poets, fiction and nonfiction writers, many who have published a number of books, a few who have yet to publish, a few who are almost strangers, several who are my closest friends, and my wife and two daughters. My community includes Tom Newkirk, who lives across the street, and other members who write in Maine, New Hampshire, Massachusetts, New York, Maryland, Georgia, Ohio, Colorado, Wyoming, Idaho, Utah, and Nova Scotia. They are the people I write *to* but not *for*. I see them as I write, read their responses to my sentences, hear their laughter, see their nodding support, but I do not write for them. They are not a committee of approval. I write for myself.

Become Your Own Best Reader

You have to absorb and respond to the criticisms of your test readers and the demands of your teacher or editor, but you have to remain as true to yourself as possible by responding in your own way, by making the final draft yours.

Be both demanding and forgiving of yourself. Try to avoid a concern with reputation and reward and focus on the draft evolving under your hand.

Read to Learn from the Draft

I believe that if I attend to the draft, read it carefully, and listen to what it says, the draft will tell me what a reader needs. I will hear the draft asking for more evidence, less description, a clear opinion, a change of pace, great detail, a more appropriate voice. The reading will tell me what works and what needs work. The draft will instruct.

Suggestion

Set the agenda for a test reader: List in writing how the reader can help you by responding to the draft. Draft the questions you hope they will answer. Find a test reader. Give the reader your draft and your questions, then invite the reader to make any other comments he or she thinks will help the draft.

Revise for Order

Now that we know the dominant meaning of the draft and have identified the audience to whom that meaning is to be delivered, we are ready to build the house of meaning.

And you, the writer, need the house of meaning as much as the reader. You have a discovery draft, a rough sketch of your writing, notes, and other research materials. Depending on the subject, those notes—mental and physical—may include books and articles you have read, your notes on them, interviews with sources, memories, observations, lab notebook entries, historical documents, reports of experiments, draft fragments of earlier writing, government reports, scholarly monographs, all in a total mess. Your mental work space looks like a construction site littered with kegs of nails, prefab windows, piles of lumber, shingles, tools, tarpaper, concrete steps going nowhere, material filled with potential.

There are two primary stages to building a written house of meaning:

- Creating a form
- Creating a structure within that form

Form is meaning. Story says there is a beginning, a middle, and an end; that action between people shapes events. Essay states there is significant information worth commentary. A lyric poem implies there is truth to be found in image and song. Description declares there is something important to describe; a report says that something has occurred that needs to be reported to a reader; argument posits that there is something to be argued over.

Structure supports the meaning. Remove your skeleton, step back, and look at yourself, a disgusting plop of skin, flesh, hair, eyes, nose, ears, and stuff. A mess. Yucckk. Call for a scoop.

Write without a skeleton and you get, you're right, a mess. An effective piece of writing has a sturdy skeleton. The skeleton connects each part of the writing so that all the parts work, developing and supporting the principal meaning of the draft.

Discovering the Form of the Draft

To build a house of meaning, we have to decide on the appropriate form of the house. Is it a two-story colonial, a ranch house or split level, city townhouse or vacation home at the lake? Form is the meaningful shape of the content, form contains the meaning. A line is drawn that includes and excludes. In revising we consider and reconsider the shape of the draft, riding circuit along the fences that include and exclude. What's in, what's out? What supports the meaning, what detracts from it? What moves the reader forward? What documents, clarifies, develops, communicates?

Internal Form

Most writers try to find the form within the draft. They read the draft to see how the content—what is being said—shapes the material, how meaning gives form to the message. If I have fallen through the ice, the form of my message is a simple yell, "Help!!!"; if I am debating the safety of the new ice with the rest of the hockey team, the form is argument; if I am remembering that debate fifty years later, the form is memoir; if I have been placed on a town committee to propose safety measures for skaters on Mill Pond, the form will be report. The material in the form, the purpose of the draft, the targeted reader, will all determine the effective form.

In the cases above, the form is clear, but many times the writer is not sure in writing the first draft what material belongs in the draft, what is the meaning of the material, the purpose in writing it, the reader who needs or wants this information.

In that case we read to see the pattern of meaning within the draft, the discovered form. Some of us call this the organic form because it appears to rise from the material. In a sense, this is an illusion, because the discovered forms have almost always been discovered years, even centuries before, but it is an important illusion—and we all live by our illusions.

A boy is supposed to have asked Michelangelo, "How did you know there was a lion in the rock?" I have the illusion I can see the lion in the rock, that I can visualize the poem, essay, textbook, academic article, newspaper column in the material of the draft.

I read loosely to see how the material seems to be arranging itself, how the voice of the text is emphasizing certain elements and passing quickly over others, what seems to belong together and what does not. It is exciting when this happens. My second novel grew out of what began as a magazine nonfiction article; I sit down to write an essay and hear a poem.

I respect my material and listen to it for what shape it seems to be developing. I think it is important to emphasize the relationship of respect writers should have toward their material. A writer should respect the integrity of the specific pieces of information collected, especially if those details contradict what the writer expected; a writer should respect the patterns into which this material arranges itself—the meaning that arises from the material—especially if it is traitor to the writer's intent; a writer should respect the message from the language—the music of the evolving text, its voice—especially if it does not say what the writer thought it would say or was saying during the writing of the draft.

It is the material, in the best writing, that determines the form.

External Form

Of course, the forms we discover have their own history. We may extend them a bit, change what is considered fashionable, but we do not invent new forms. Recently I attended a seminar in which we read Dickens's *Bleak House*. I was surprised at how different it was from the contemporary fiction I am used to reading today.

It was enormous, filled with many characters. The pace was leisurely, the parts of the fiction—the introduction of characters, the descriptive passages—were not integrated with the rest of the text as they would be today. The commentary of the author intruded, and the language was formal, wordy, inflated by today's standards. *Bleak House* is a great novel but not a contemporary one; it is a novel of its own time. I was struck by how much those of us who write fiction have been influenced by the cinema, even by TV commercials. Dickens would write differently if he were alive today.

But Dickens was a storyteller, and all the narrative techniques are there. We wear different literary clothes but we tell stories through characters who interact with one another in scenes that exist in a place, and each scene solves a problem and establishes a new one to propel the narrative forward. *Bleak House* and tomorrow's best-selling novel are written in the same narrative tradition.

Subconscious Tradition

When we write we follow, often without knowing it, our literary traditions. These traditions evolve over time in response to need. Our ancestors, staggering back to the cave after the hunt, needed to report what they found and did not find, what trends affected the survival of the family. They needed to make sense, as I did in World War II, of combat that was terrifying, confusing, meaningless. They needed to instruct the young in the techniques of tracking and the kill that were successful. They needed to celebrate and mourn, reward and comfort, plan and organize, entertain and motivate. The forms we use today, influenced along the way by movable type and the TV sound bite, are still essentially the same.

We can understand the forms of writing by putting ourselves within the world in which the form is used. I used to have my beginning journalism students consider the conditions of journalism: the arrival of immense amounts of confusing material; a brief time in which to absorb, select, and write; a busy readership that needed, in a hurry, a momentary understanding of events. The students would create traditional news style—and know it far better than when I taught it.

You can create your own traditional forms of discourse by considering the material, the reader, and how it can best be transmitted from writer to reader. You will, of course, be influenced by the traditions you already know but may not know that you know. You know narrative from street-corner anecdote, from TV and radio, from the Bible and other books, even from comic books and romance novels.

As a writer I am aware of many traditions, but when I face a new task I look first at the task. I have been hired as a ghost writer by corporations, and when I accept an assignment I do not first look at what has been done in the past but at the message and its receiver. Then, when I have "created" a form to fit the task, I study published forms to test my invented form against the lessons of experience.

Conscious Tradition

When facing a writing task you have not attempted before, you can find out the forms that have been successful in the past by looking at books that analyze and explain argument, business writing, screen writing, science writing, writing nursing and police reports, news writing, fiction and poetry writing, scholarly writing, writing criticism and speeches. Such books conduct autopsies of successful writing in that form, revealing the conventions—the tricks of the trade—that have worked in the past.

It is also possible to take a piece of writing you like—or one the audience you are trying to reach trusts and respects—and analyze to see what the author has done. Let me give you an immediate example from my own professional experience. While I was writing this chapter Marjorie Pritchard, editor of the page opposite the editorials in the *Boston Globe,* called and asked if I would write a six-hundred-word piece about the eighties—the "Reagan Years"—for an end-of-the-decade issue from the point of view of those over age sixty. I was flattered and intrigued. I knew my feelings about this decade were complicated, but I didn't know why. I wrote and rewrote the piece instinctively—I have internalized the traditions I follow—but now I will go back through this brief essay with you to show the traditions I followed and show you how you can analyze a piece of writing to learn the lessons you can apply to your own writing task. I do not see this brief newspaper commentary as *the* ideal. I do see it as a professional piece of work that is well made, and it will be interesting to me to see what traditions I followed. You will discover that it does not take great intellect to see what works in a piece of writing.

My task was clear: to sum up a decade from the point of view of someone who was in his sixties at its end. I chose to be personal. I could have stood back and commented from a historical distance; I am trained to do that, but I am more comfortable—and more effective, I think—when I move in close and look at one life, the one I am most familiar with. Readers of my specifics will recall their own, I hope.

> Over sixty, each morning walk is a celebration. Another sunrise, another hike by the Mill Pond, another quiet hour in which to anticipate the day and, often, to put this day in the context of so many days past.

■   The form and tone of this essay is familiar. My style is not E.B. White's, but I realize I have been influenced and inspired by his work. I am establishing a mood of personal reflection. I establish my angle of vision; I am looking back from the perspective of one who is over sixty.

I do not like the terms *topic sentence* and *thesis statement* because they can limit the writer prematurely, but here I establish what I am doing as I "put this day in the context of so many days past." This first paragraph prepares the reader for what is to come.   ■

> Marching along this winter morning, I relive the Battle of the Bulge I survived by luck, not soldierly skills. The GI bill allowed me, a high school dropout and flunkout, the college education

my parents could not afford. And that education allowed me to have a vocation instead of a job, like my father.

■ It is fascinating to look back and discover what I was doing by instinct. No, more than that, I was discovering what I had to say. It looks, from this perspective, as if I were supporting what comes later but, no, I am writing the support; later I will write what the support leads toward.

Here, in terms of form, I am developing the paragraph, reporting on my thoughts. To understand my feelings about the eighties I have to establish my personal context for them. I discovered the idea of luck here, but I will pick up that thread and use it later. ■

Now, the decade of the eighties has allowed me more financial comfort than I had any reason to expect. I live where I can walk by a Mill Pond and return to a single-family home. I tell Jessie, the neighbor dog greeting me as I near home, that I made it, Jessie, made it into the middle class.

■ In the third paragraph I return to the assigned topic, the eighties, and describe my situation, putting it in the context of my childhood. E.B. White is a more graceful writer than I, but I am using his light tone. It takes the pompous ego out of bragging about my success by my bragging to a dog.

My paragraphs are short because a line of typewritten copy becomes two lines in a newspaper and ten lines of type for a newspaper reader become a formidable block of type. ■

I have a wife who is a closer friend than the lonely teenager I was could have imagined, two daughters, and a son-in-law who are friends and the memories of twenty years of companionship with the daughter who left early.

■ Notice how apparent form is? You can take a piece of writing and easily see how it is formed. No mystery. Here I am documenting my good fortune in specific terms. ■

Stepping from the shower, I surprise myself with the zipper scar of my 1987 bypass, the fashionable operation for mature males in my neighborhood. I had my father's heart attack on schedule but modern medicine gave me the operation he could not have—or imagine.

■ More good fortune, told in active specific terms that relate to the eighties when I had my bypass. In the sixties that was not available. Maybe I should add "in the sixties" to the last line? ■

I retired from the university early, a couple of years early, and I'm still able to write—and get paid for it. Well, not the poetry, but I'm getting some poems published, fulfilling my under-graduate dream.

■ I hope in using specific details of my life that I will cause readers to translate my specifics into their own. My target, for this piece, is the successful over sixty. I will articulate the unspoken feelings of some, if I am lucky, and cause a few more to have feelings or thoughts. To do this, I have to get them nodding in agreement, I have to earn their trust that I know their world. ■

I live a fortunate life and I know how lucky I am. On my walk this chill morning I passed our small town's homeless man. I nodded, but he veered off, striding to some imaginary meeting. I have benefited from the Reagan years that deinstitutionalized him—a body-count type of word that hides his pain and our obligation. I count my tax advantages and feel guilty.

■ Again, I did this instinctively but this is the seventh paragraph of a twelve-paragraph piece—exactly half-way through. I feel I've got the reader's trust and iden-tification, now I turn up the heat. But I do it with narrative, with the kind of detail that most Americans in the late eighties are seeing and most of the time try-ing to ignore. Now I force the reader to pay attention.

This is a transition paragraph, a turning point, a fulcrum. Notice the movement of thought represented in the change from the first sentence of the paragraph and the last that echoes the first, but with a crucial twist. ■

I'd like to believe I have received the proper reward for a life of hard work, but I know I have not. Like the times I fell down out of clumsiness in battle and missed my bullet. I know I have lived in the right country at the right time. I haven't worked as hard or long as my ancestors who labored on farms in the Hebrides and sent their profits to the absentee landlords in England, or those who were sucked into the linen mills, or the one who a genealogical search revealed ended up in the work-house in his seventies.

■ Here I make a point and document it.
　　　I also employ an effective argumentative strategy. Again it is instinctive, as it may be with you when arguing with a parent. I don't point the finger at someone else, but stay true to the reflective tone I have established and reflect on my life. If I have caused the readers to identify with me they may be taken where they do not expect or want to go, questioning the causes of their success, not hard work rewarded but luck. ■

I may have, I often think these days, lived in the best of times. We know too well the problems and the vacuum of positive leadership from the right, left, or middle, from the town council to the State House to the White House. Give the problems your own priorities:

■ Turn up the heat another notch. And I try to include people of right and left from local to national governments. ■

The homeless. AIDS. Ozone. Pollution of ocean, sky, and land. Drugs. The cannibalization of a capitalistic system to satisfy immediate greed. An unexpected increase in racial and religious prejudice. An unwillingness to pay for an effective education. Wasteful overdevelopment of mallcondomallcondos. Fast food with indestructible packaging. A worry that peace may break out and our most feared enemy will turn out to be ourselves.

■ Bang. Bang. Bang. Now I hit them fast and hard in specific terms. ▪

And behind the lack of leadership, a meanness, a shirking of responsibility by those, like myself, who have made it. A lack of concern for those who have not had our luck. And an unwillingness to accept that it is luck, not virtue. A habit of blaming the victim for the crime, the sick for their disease, the unfortunate for their misfortune.

■ I go behind the specific problems to attitudes that are my real target. If the form of my argument works, I will bring readers along with me. If I have anticipated my readers' unspoken concerns, and articulated their unspoken thoughts and feelings, I will cause some of them to change their attitudes, at least a little bit. I would not have accomplished this by a frontal attack that would have put the readers on the defensive. ▪

I put Mozart on the CD player, sit back, put my feet up, enjoy my view of my private woods, well-to-do from the economic policies that reward the fortunate and ignore the rest; entering the nineties worried but comfortable, guilty but passive, concerned but detached.

■ I put the blame squarely on me. I am not faking that. This is how I feel, but I hope that some readers will hear themselves in me and change their views.
Also note that I do not come up with easy answers. I am merely articulating the unresolved conflict within many of us. I am defining the central tension I feel that I benefit from the political policies and social attitudes with which I disagree. ▪

No magic. Just a careful reading of a text, asking what the writer is doing, paragraph by paragraph. An effective piece of writing—one that works—will stand up to this type of scrutiny and instruct a writer who needs to understand the form. The traditions of form exist in those scholarly texts that preserve and sometimes evangelize them, they are preserved in the texts themselves as I have just demonstrated, and in a third place: the reader's expectations.

Reader Expectation

"Read me a story," the child demands, insisting on the story that was read last night—and the night before that and the night before that and the night before . . . . The child wants the familiar scary part, the familiar rescue.

We are the same way. We turn to the predictable situation comedy or ask a friend, "What happened Saturday night?" knowing that friend will come up with another tale of romantic hope and comic failure. We delight in the familiar pace of the story, the expected punch line.

We all live in a world of expected patterns at school, at work, at home, and it is true of what we hear and what we read. We have expectations of story, lab report, argument, essay, book or movie review, business letter, and personal letter.

Riding the Wave of Expectation

The experienced writer anticipates the reader's expectations and makes use of them, developing, pacing, and voicing the draft to the reader's desires. If the boss wants specific facts, the reader delivers specific facts; if the reader expects understanding, the writer understands; if the reader will only consider an argument that appeals to the brain, the writer serves up thought; if the reader wants emotion, the writer provides emotional material; if the reader is busy, the writer is brief.

The writer becomes the reader, imagines what the reader expects, and delivers in many forms of writing. Each form the writer uses has its own pattern of reader expectation, and since we are readers as well as writers, we can predict those expectations.

Writing against Expectation

Some of the most effective writing, however, is written against the reader's expectations. The reader expects a sermon and receives a humorous story; the reader expects humor and receives a government report filled with facts that the reader slowly discovers is hilarious; the reader expects an emotional argument and is delivered a list of hard, cold facts; the audience expects a high-flown political speech full of grand clichés and hears a quiet, honest piece of autobiography; the reader of an annual report expects statistics and is taken on a walk through a manufacturing plant.

You can work against reader expectation when the draft communicates significant information in the manner most appropriate to that information, but it is important, in some way, to allow the reader to know that you know the reader's expectations and are contradicting them on purpose. It may be done directly: "No, not the same story tonight but a different story that tells about another three bears"; "No, I'm not going to tell you about Saturday night. Just read this letter I got this morning"; "Our annual reports are usually filled with unreadable statistics, but this year in our company history we think it important for you to understand how we have spent your money to clean up environmental problems and be a better neighbor."

You may be able to accomplish this more subtly, but the reader who comes to the page with an expectation—and all readers do—deserves a response to that expectation. If you don't anticipate readers' expectations, they will go away early and go away mad, and you aren't an effective writer if your readers leave and don't turn the page.

Suggestion

Make a quick list of all the forms your draft might take and then select the one most appropriate to your meaning and your audience; then list the reader's expectations from that form and note any way you might write against those expectations.

Design Your Own Form

The writer is the architect of the house of meaning and the writer works as an architect: selecting from the inventory of traditional forms; discovering the form that is buried in the drafting-board sketch or draft; or designing a new form to fit this particular situation.

The first way, selection of traditional forms, is most commonly taught because there is a significant body of knowledge going back to the Greeks—and beyond—that can be described and understood in a historical context. Students and teachers think all the writer has to do is choose a traditional form and fit the material into it, and some writing, indeed, reads as if that happened.

I, like most writers, prefer to reverse order and start with the discovered form and then consider designing a form if that is necessary. Of course both are an illusion. Few, if any, of us actually discover a form. Scholars can see in our published drafts the history of rhetorical forms. But these are significant illusions, illusions to live by, or at least, to write by.

But we, as writers, have looked to the key elements of the communication act and at least adapted the forms we know to the particular message being sent to a particular reader.

The Discovered Form

To discover the organic or natural form that lies within a draft you can read the draft quickly, trying to visualize the outlines of the piece, its horizons or boundary fences. There may be several forms in a draft. It may tell a story and use narrative techniques, try to persuade the reader and use some of the strategies of argument, relate facts in a manner appropriate to a scientific report. All these techniques might be used in a magazine article on an environmental problem. But the overall form would be an investigative piece of magazine journalism. Your job as a writer is to discover the form that contains and communicates the message effectively.

The Invented Form

The invented form is forged from three principal forces, and once those forces are identified the process of invention is usually easy, a matter of simple logic. Usually the inexperienced writer invents—or reinvents—the form after a first draft and the experienced writer before the first draft, but the process of design is the same.

Message

What is said comes first. The message itself—*I need money*—is a force in determining the form. Each message may need a special container that will carry it efficiently to the reader.

Purpose

The purpose of the writer is another force that shapes form. The purpose of the message—*I need money*—may be to get sympathy from a friend, to delay suit from someone to whom you owe money, to make someone pay up who owes you money, or to negotiate a loan from a parent, bank, or college financial-aid officer.

Reader

The one who is to receive the message also exerts a profound influence on the form. An appeal that works with a mother may not work with a father, a friend who owes you money may not be influenced by your good grades, but a financial-aid officer may be affected by that information.

In each of these cases, of course, there may be many levels. You may have several messages to deliver—I don't want to see you again unless . . . and if we do get together again we must be sure . . . and I understand that I must try and . . . and, If I do that, you should . . . . You may have more than one purpose: to show the boss what procedure could save money at the check-out counter, and what a bright person you are, and how hard you work, and that you deserve a raise and more hours. You may have more than one reader: I am writing this textbook for you—and your teachers and for teachers who teach teachers and for writers or potential writers. It can help to know these levels, but we must, in each case, establish a priority if we are to develop an effective form and structure, if we are to build an effective house of meaning.

Create an Effective Design

It is a simple, logical matter to create an effective design, a rhetorical form that is custom made to communicate a message to a listener and accomplish a clear purpose. Remember you have been using speech to persuade, report, entertain, communicate since before you started school. You know many of the forms of our literary heritage, you simply don't know the names scholars use to describe them—and that doesn't matter in the designing process.

Put the following headings across the top of a sheet or pad of paper, even at the top of your computer display screen.

Message ⟶ Purpose ⟶   FORM   ⟵ Reader

Write a brief description of your message in the left hand column, add a statement of purpose in the second column, then jump over Form and write a brief description of your reader. *Then* consider the forms that might deliver that message to that reader and accomplish your purpose. It may be the form you have used in the first draft, the form you used with some modifications, a form you have read and written before, a way—new to you—of delivering a message to a reader.

Here are some examples of how this method might work:

Message ⟶	Purpose ⟶	FORM	⟵ Reader
I have two years' experience waiting on tables, one cooking. Want summer job as night-shift manager.	To get better summer job.	• Letter saying how much you love Rock Beach, how much fun you had there as a kid. • Letter telling how much college costs. • Copy of short story about funny things that happened where you worked last summer. • Letter describing experience in businesslike terms, including references and	Ms. Gates, owner. Tough, suspicious of college kids.

Message ⟶   Purpose ⟶   FORM   ⟵ Reader

> plan to go into hotel management.
> • Memo based on observation as a customer making specific suggestions about what night manager should do. Add a brief resume.

No mystery here. The last one gives the writer the best shot at the job. Try this yourself. The creation of an effective form is a matter of logic. During the oil crisis in the seventies a corporation hired me to write their appeal to a government agency for an increase in propane. I knew nothing about the business, but I had the form I have given you. I described their needs, the purpose—to get more propane—and imagined a board that was receiving appeals from industry all across the country. I drafted an appeal that gave them more propane— and was suggested as a model by the government for other companies. No magic. You have the skills in hand to create a form that will work for you.

Using a Traditional Form

As I have said, I think it is more effective to design your own form because you have to do some careful thinking about your message, purpose, and reader, but the forms you "invent" are usually on the shelf in the rhetorician's warehouse. They may be under such general headings as narrative, argument, report; or they may be categorized by purpose: to persuade, to tell a story, to explain, or to instruct. The forms may also be in a specialized warehouse: chemistry lab experiment, sales report, U.S. Army training manual, history term paper, nursing log, engineering field journal. The list goes on and on.

In whatever field you study, there will be forms that you can try on for size, adapt, and modify to fit your message, purpose, and reader. As you write, you will develop your inventory of forms with which you are familiar, but you should never forget that you can invent the forms you need when you face a new writing task.

Suggestion

Use the chart on page 100–101 and design a form that will carry your meaning to your reader effectively.

Keeping in; Cutting out

The effective writer creates from an abundance of information, an abundance of thought, an abundance of feeling. The experienced writer feels the same panic in facing this abundance as the inexperienced writer, but the published writer knows that feeling of going down for the third time under the ocean of information, ideas, and emotions is natural and essential.

Effective writing is the product of a full inventory of material from which the writer can choose the material from which to construct a sturdy piece of prose. The writer has to be able to pick the appropriate quotation, the revealing detail, the precise word, the supporting melody, the accurate insight, the fitting feeling, the documenting statistic from a warehouse of potential material. And, therefore, the revising writer has to master this abundance, making effective use of what is on hand to discover, clarify, and communicate meaning.

People imagine the artist—writer, painter, composer— as a dreamer, a flaky sort of person who floats a foot-and-a-half above reality, hardly ever touching ground. And writers like to encourage this romantic Bohemian air. Let us not examine too closely why I avoid ties, wear jeans to at least semi-formal affairs, cover my chin with a beard. But the fact is that artists are hard-headed executives, skilled at making the tough decisions of selection. Go behind the beard and beret and you'll see a factory manager, a battlefield surgeon, a scientist directing an experiment with cool detachment.

What Is Saved

All that is saved in the draft is the material that gives the form shape and meaning. Each detail, each word, phrase, line, paragraph must move the meaning forward.

When revising, the writer must, with a cold eye and an icy heart, examine each piece of information the writer has collected, each lovely phrase the writer has created, and save only those that clarify, develop, support, communicate the meaning.

We are all possessive of what we write. We are aware of the time we have invested in research, planning, and drafting. We are secretly paternal and maternal, proud of the offspring we have produced. But no matter how startling the information, how clever our words, we can only include that which relates to our meaning.

What Is Discarded

Remember Isaac Bashevis Singer's wastebasket. He knows what isn't, is. The marble chipped away is an essential part of the statue. Art is selection and what is discarded reveals what remains.

What is thrown into the wastebasket is not wasted. The material not used—that fascinating specific, the unexpected quote, the phrase that once seemed to illuminate, the concept that once appeared to bring all the elements together—led to what was used, what is in the process of revealing meaning, and what will be shared in the final draft.

Suggestion

Make a list or go through the draft and mark what must be saved and what now can be let go. Notice how this act of house cleaning simplifies what you have to work on in the revision ahead.

Discovering Your Structure

The architect not only decides on the exterior of the house but creates a floor plan. Rooms must have doors so they can be used, floors must be reached by stairs. The house of meaning needs an internal structure. You have written in some order, consciously and unconsciously, and the first step in revising for structure is to discover the order the draft has taken.

Reveal the Structure

To reveal the structure, you have to perform an autopsy and reveal the skeleton of logic—or illogic—that lies beneath the prose.

Outline *after* Writing

The most effective way to discover the skeleton is to write an outline. What? After you have written a draft? Yes. In fact, that may be the most effective time to use an outline. Read through the draft and write down the major points you have made and the minor points under each one. You can get fancy and use alphabetical and Roman numeral headings or use a numerical system popular with most computer people, but you don't have to worry about which system to use. Just write the major points in the left margin and indent the supporting points under them—and further supporting points, if necessary, indented under those.

Here's my outline for the revision of this chapter that combines two chapters, one on form and another on structure in the first draft of the book. I keep this to the left of my computer as I write. It is a map that tells me where I am and where I'm going as I revise, but unlike the map of the Atlantic coast near my home I can change this map. If I need an island, I can stick one in; if an island is in the way, I can take it out.

CHAPTER 6
Revise for Order

Discovering the Form of the Draft

Internal Form
External Form
   Subconscious Tradition
   Conscious Tradition
   Reader Expectation
      Riding the Wave of Expectation
      Writing Against Expectation

Design Your Own Form

The Discovered Form
The Invented Form
   Message
   Purpose
   Reader
Create an Effective Design
Using a Traditional Form

Keeping in; Cutting out

What Is Saved
What Is Discarded

Discovering Your Structure within the Form

Reveal the Structure
   Outline after Writing
Adapt the Structure

Designing an Effective Structure

Focus
Order
   Opening
   Turning Points
   Ending
Documentation
Pace
Proportion

You'll notice that those are the heads that appear in the chapter. That's the way I write a textbook. I write out the heads—the skeleton—playing with them until I get them right for me. Then I write the draft and the heads continue to change. Some heads or sections are dropped, others demand to be written and added. When I am done, I print them out to see the skeleton by itself and to guide me in revision.

There's no mystery about this process but you'll find it is a thinking activity and one helpful to you as a writer. Writing out the skeleton you may discover:

- The order is wrong. It doesn't serve the reader.
- There are parts that aren't needed and can be cut.
- There are new parts needed that must be added.
- Some subsections need to be more important.
- Some sections need to shrink and fit another head.

Adapt the Structure

What you have been doing with your fiddling around is adapting the structure you have to your message, audience, and form. You can usually cut and paste many parts of the draft or move them around on computer disk so that the structure you discovered by drafting the piece is refined and developed.

> ### Suggestion
>
> Write down the heads for the sections of your draft. There are always sections or small units of writing within any draft, even a one-page essay or a poem.

■ I started my writing this morning by rereading a draft of a poem, seeing imaginary heads and realized it needed to be broken into four stanzas. I went back to the poem and put the heads in. I was interested in the way it helped me to see the poem anew. Later, with the help of a poetry group I belong to, I discovered the title was one of the heads and made other changes that

I think made the poem better. This is the kind of play
in the search for meaning that writers engage in.

On Leave from Death

The Dream

It is Lee, trying not to wake her parents,
tiptoeing up the outside edge of the stairs,
home late from waitressing. I wake my wife
but it is not Lee. I do not say who I heard
so gentle on the stairs. It is better the dead
remain in the grave. But they refuse.

The Dead Return

Butler Mitchell, dead at twelve of polio,
escapes from the long black Packard hearse
that drove so slowly from the church. He races
his bike over to my house at night. He is always
twelve and I am an old man he does not know.
The dream runs backwards and the fragments

Death's Innocence

of earth, blood, bone, his left hand, reassemble
into Joe who squats beside me before the shell
arrives. Returning in a dream, he is surprised
at this old man straining at his duty. Leonard
looks up from making a May sky with watercolor
and jokes about Alden. I cannot tell him

The Living's Secrets

Alden too is gone. The living have our secrets,
let the dead return at night. They vacation here,
trying not to wake us on the stairs, ready
to bike away a Saturday, joke about the crazy
sergeant, capture one more sky with the wide
brush I touch where it remains in my drawer.

■ And now the version free of the heads. I found myself
using three-line stanzas rather than six; it seemed to
tighten the poem and clarify my meaning. ■

Death's Innocence

It is Lee, trying not to wake her parents,
tiptoeing up the outside edge of the stairs,
home late from waitressing. I wake my wife

but it is not Lee. I do not say who I heard
so gentle on the stairs. It is better the dead
remain in the grave. But they refuse.

Butler Mitchell, dead at twelve of polio,
escapes from the long black Packard hearse
that drove so slowly from the church. He races

his bike over to my house at night. He is always
twelve and I am an old man he does not know.
The film runs backwards and the fragments

of earth, blood, bone, his left hand, reassemble
into Joe who squats beside me before the shell
arrives. Returning, he is always surprised

at this old man straining at his duty. Leonard
looks up from making a May sky with watercolor
and jokes about Alden. I cannot tell him

Alden too is gone. The living have our secrets,
let the dead return at night. They vacation here,
trying not to wake us on the stairs.

■ It always helps to see the units within the writing that
lead to the development and communication of the
meaning of the entire draft. ■

Designing an Effective Structure

Sometimes you may have to design a new structure to support
the form you have chosen for your text. This is an easy, logical
task, and the time spent in developing an effective structure is
worthwhile because it will make the writing easier—and more
effective.

Focus

What is the *one* thing you want to say, Murray?

That is a question I keep asking myself. Of course, I know I may say a number of things in a piece of writing, but one has to dominate, and everything in the piece has to support or relate to that one thing. I may not know that one thing before I write the draft or it may change as I write the draft, but at the time of revision I need to know the focus of the piece. That is the point at which I begin to design my structure. I write that one thing down in a sentence or less.

Order

An effective design has an order or sequence of information that will draw the reader through the draft.

Opening

First, obviously, is the opening. The first line or paragraph draws the reader into the point and points the direction in which it is going. I am willing to try a dozen, two dozen, three dozen first lines to discover a line that will both attract the reader and show me where the draft is going.

Here is an example of how I might work on the first sentence of an essay exploring my feelings about football to discover the trail I might follow in writing the draft. This trail should attract the reader as well.

- I am proud—and embarrassed—that I played football.
- In the closet the other day I found the sweater with the letter I earned playing varsity football. It doesn't fit anymore and I wondered just how well it fit then.
- I confess that the sport I like best to watch is football—that violent, militaristic game that is so typically American.

Note that each opening contains a tension that may cause the writer to write—and the reader to read.

Turning Points

I list the main points, usually three to five, *then* order them in a logical sequence. I don't use general categories—urban problems—but specifics—murders up 321 percent—to mark the main points. That helps me see what I am going to write and how it relates to the rest of the piece. I need to get them down before I juggle them around into the most effective order.

What is that order? It depends, but one way I discover it is to anticipate the reader's questions and then answer them in the order they will be asked.

Ending

The well-structured draft has an ending that resolves the issues in the piece. That doesn't mean wrapping everything up with a pretty ribbon, but it does mean that the reader has a sense of completion, that the reader knows more about the subject than when he or she began reading. Usually this means an echo back to what was said first.

Of course a change in the ending may affect the beginning, and I will have to change the opening or the order in the middle. I have to work back and forth until I have a sturdy structure that will stand up to a critical reading.

Documentation

Next, I use my own shorthand—cri fcts (crime statistics), anec cops (police anecdote), com qte (commissioner's quotation)—to indicate the documentation I plan to use to support each point and advance the dominant meaning of the draft.

Pace

Now I can scan my notes and estimate the pace of the draft, an important element in the designing of an effective structure. If I move too fast the reader will get lost and not have time to absorb and understand each point before moving on to the next one; if I move too slowly the reader will be bored and stop reading.

Proportion

A related question involves the proportions of the elements in the design. I may see that I have a great deal of documentation

for my second point, none for the third that is equally important. The reader will be uncomfortable if I have five pages on
one point, five sentences on another, unless those proportions
are appropriate to the meaning of the draft.

Now that the house of meaning has been designed, the
writer is ready to deal with the specific questions of specific
information and language. Until now, the writer could not be
sure what information was needed and how the voice should be
tuned, but now that the frame of the draft is up, the writer can
move to finish revising the draft.

Suggestion

Take your draft and design your own house of meaning.
Decide on the form, the exterior design of the house, and
then construct a floor plan so that the reader will move
easily through the rooms.

7

Revise for Evidence

Writers don't write with words.

Writers write with information—accurate, specific, significant information. It is essential to the craft of revision to consider the information communicated in the draft. Words are the symbols for information, and when there is no information behind the words the draft is like a check with no money in the account: worthless.

Effective writing serves the reader information the reader can use to understand the world, to think more clearly, to make better decisions, to learn, to act, to appreciate and enjoy life, to become an authority in the eyes of those around the reader. The list of reasons readers want and need information is long. Effective writing is constructed from sturdy bits of information.

The Importance of Information

It is normal for young writers—and some not so young—to become infatuated with words. The condition is called "word drunk." The writer staggers down the page, spouting words that may, accidentally, sound wonderful but say nothing. But most readers do not want a word-drunk writer any more than they want a shaky-handed surgeon.

Reader Satisfaction

Readers hunger for information. They want the images and facts, revealing details and interesting quotations, amazing statistics and insights that make them see, feel, and know their world better than they did before the reading.

The information-rich writer is an authority, and reading makes the reader an authority: The reader broadcasts the new information to family, colleagues, friends. A good piece of writing ignites a chain reaction of communication as reader becomes an author (an authority) and the listener in turn becomes an author when the information is passed on.

Most of the writing that satisfies us as readers has served us an abundance of information.

Establishes Authority

Readers believe specific information. If you want to lie, lie with statistics. Precise information makes the reader believe that you know your stuff. But serve up one piece of precise information that the reader knows is wrong and the reader won't believe anything in your text.

Accurate information is the reason that readers trust the writer; inaccurate information is the reason that readers mistrust the writer. Readers test the draft by noting the information that relates to their world. When I read something about a newspaper or a university I am especially critical. If I think the writer is on target I trust the writer's comments about institutions I do not know well, but if the writer's comments do not fit my knowledge of newspapers or universities then I suspect everything the writer says.

Produces Lively Writing

"How can I make my writing lively? It is dull, dull, dull."

Yesterday I was asked that question and I answered, "By concrete details more than anything else. Lively writing is

specific, not vague, abstract, and general. It builds the generalizations on the page and in the reader's mind from specific
pieces of information that surprise and delight the reader."

Suggestion

Take a newspaper or magazine story about a subject you
know—surfing, working in a supermarket, life in a soror-
ity, living in Chicago—and read it, circling the specific
pieces of information you know are true Cross out the ones
you know are untrue or questionable. Then read the piece
again to see the effect of your trust or distrust of the writer.

The Qualities of Effective Information

Effective information is information the reader uses successfully. A manual tells the reader how to solve a problem with
computer software; an editorial makes the reader change a
vote; a biography puts a historical figure in perspective;
a literature text illuminates a poem; the poem makes the
reader see the woods the reader passes every day with increased perception.

Accuracy

One of the reasons readers respect specific information is that
the author takes the risk of being specific. Much of what pours
through our ears is purposely vague, general, abstract; the
writer uses political language that can't be nailed down, information for which the writer is not accountable. Specific writing
is unusual, and readers like it, *but* it must be correct. One slip,
as previously said, and the reader will not trust anything the
writer says.

Factual Accuracy
The first accuracy is the truth of the fact: the number of miles in
the marathon, the cost of the school bond issue, the day of the

Battle of Gettysburg, the ingredients in the formula and their precise amounts, what the president actually said in the speech—all must be right.

These facts can be checked with authoritative sources and should be. Often the writer will check the source with another source; just because a statement is in print doesn't mean it is a fact.

Some questions you can ask of a fact, then check and recheck if the answer is not "yes," are:

- Does it make any sense?
- Does it seem possible from what you know of the subject?
- Is it consistent with other facts you know are correct, does it fit the pattern?
- If this statement is true, does it change other facts in the draft—or the meaning of the draft?

Of course, the most interesting and significant facts will not get a simple "yes," but those pieces of information will have to face the skepticism of the reader. They deserve to be checked and rechecked.

Contextual Accuracy

It is not enough, however, to have simple accuracy. Specific information has enormous power; it affects everything around it and is affected by everything around it. When I was at *Time* magazine each word in every story had a dot placed over it by a researcher. The color of the dot indicated the kind of checking that had verified the accuracy of the detail. And the magazine would go to extraordinary means to check the fact.

This emphasis on accuracy is good, but it can lead to technical accuracy—the color of the woman executive's business suit was mauve, a bluish purple—and contextual inaccuracy—by leaving out the fact she was a specialist in international trade brought in to save the corporation. The emphasis on the color of her suit was sexist and trivialized her.

The writer has the responsibility to make sure the information in the text is *accurate in context*. That is a far more difficult, and more important, task than just checking the number of pork pies at a church supper. Some questions that may help you test the contextual accuracy of a specific piece of information are:

- What does this detail mean to the reader? What message does it deliver to the reader?
- What does this specific make the reader think? Feel?
- What impression is conveyed by this specific and the information that surrounds it?
- What is the pattern of meaning being built by this piece of information and the specifics that come before and after it?
- Is this piece of information accurate in context?

You are using specific information to construct a meaning and you have the obligation to make that meaning true.

Specificity

We like specific information because it catches our eye, or ear; sets off chain reactions of memory or imagination; gives us something to play with; makes us think and feel.

The Disadvantages of General Information

Meanings, feelings, ideas, generalizations, theories, abstractions are all important. We use them in writing but we are fortunate when we can cause them to happen in the reader's mind because of what we have said on the page. The details are arranged in a pattern, and that pattern makes the reader construct a meaning or experience a feeling. We cannot usually construct a meaning from generalities. There is nothing there to cause a thought. There is just someone else's thought to be accepted or rejected. It is given to us without documentation. We can't see backstage to discover—and evaluate—how it was put together.

Writers—and politicians, corporate executives, educational administrators, bureaucrats—often use generalizations to avoid responsibility. You can't nail a generalization down. Watch a presidential press conference—either party will do.

Undocumented generalizations—those that are not built out of accurate, checkable, specific information in front of your eyes—are weak, flabby, vague, dull. And the writing is . . . .

The Advantages of Revealing Details
Revealing details expose the subject; they connect with other details to construct an opinion, argument, theory, poem, story, report that can be studied, challenged, tested.

The details themselves have power. "The mayor won" is not equal to "the mayor won five votes to her opponent's one." And details can make the reader think beyond the end of the sentence: "The first black to be elected mayor won with 71 percent of the white vote." Or make the reader feel: "In her victory statement she thanked her husband, her children, her parents, her campaign workers and then lifted Soozie, her seeing-eye dog, up on her hind legs so she could acknowledge the cheers of the mayor's supporters."

Significance

Effective information is significant. If the new mayor had a dog named Soozie that would mean nothing, but the fact that it is a seeing-eye dog makes a statement about the possibilities for the handicapped—a term the mayor never uses—and implies that her administration will pay attention to that minority as well.

Resonance
A powerful detail has resonance, it gives off an explosion of implication in the reader's mind. The mayor reminds the audience that she went to school in this city, but that although each year the white high school students elected a mayor who served for a day in City Hall, she was *not* allowed to serve when her black classmates elected her their mayor.

That piece of information resonates. The reader can imagine how she felt then and how she feels now, can imagine the struggle that put her where she is now, can imagine how many other talented citizens did not and do not have the chance to serve, can imagine the changes that allow this to happen and the changes that need to take place.

Connection
The information you choose should make significant connections in the writer's mind and the reader's.

With Topic

The information should relate to the topic and advance its meaning in the reader's mind. Often writers collect interesting information and they can't let go of it. The more interesting it is the more it draws the reader's mind away from the message you are delivering. Each specific should amplify, clarify, extend the topic.

With Other Information

The specific details should work with the other pieces of information in the text. They should build toward an increasing understanding of the meaning your draft is delivering to the reader. Some will increase the impact of the other details; other specifics will qualify or limit the meaning that is building up. During revision you have the opportunity to check on these relationships.

With Reader

The information you choose to use should relate to the reader. Both the type of information—statistics, anecdotes, quotations—and the meaning the information bears should appeal to the reader. What will persuade one reader may turn another off. It is your job to select appropriate information from which to construct your draft.

Fairness

When I started to publish, my editors would talk about objectivity. Today that is a term we rarely use. We have realized that writing is a craft of selection and we cannot—and should not—be detached and unconcerned about our topics. We must, however, attempt to be fair.

The best way to evaluate the fairness of a draft is to stand back and become a person in the piece of writing or someone who is affected by it. What would you think if you were in the piece or if your reputation were affected by its publication?

> ### Suggestion
>
> To reveal to yourself the power of specific information, write a general statement about someone you know— "Jennifer is a nice person"—and then list twenty specifics that document her niceness. Now change the statement by adding "not" before "a nice person." Write down another twenty specifics. Now write a paragraph that is fair, documenting the strengths and weaknesses of the person with specific, accurate details.

Basic Forms of Information

We deal with information all the time, but we don't think of it as information we might use to construct a piece of writing. It may be a good idea to remind ourselves of the common forms of information.

Fact: A precise piece of information that can be documented by independent sources. Linda J. Stone was **elected governor**.

Statistic: A numerical fact. The governor received **5,476,221** votes.

Quotation: **"The first Monday of every month the door to my office will be open to any citizen who wishes to see me."**

Anecdote: **Governor-elect Stone drove the family car, a five-year-old Ford station wagon with 137,422 miles on it, to election headquarters herself**.

Descriptive detail: She held high the **old-fashioned wooden clip board** she carried during the campaign on which she had made notes on what individual citizens told her during the daily kaffeeklatches she held in private homes, offices, schools, and factories.

Authoritative report: In her acceptance speech, Governor-elect Stone cited the **Newkirk Report that called for small classes in the public school system and a paid-for-by-the-state system of summer retraining for teachers**.

Common information: **The governor-elect of this state is immediately given a State Police driver and an official
limousine.**

These are just a few of the most common forms of information. There are obviously many more, and I have used a
journalistic example common to all of us. Each academic discipline, each corporation, each profession, each government
agency will have its own basic inventory of information forms.
Most of them will, however, fit these patterns. The literary
scholar will have many quotations from the work studied and
from its critics; the economist will cite many statistics; the
physicist will have many facts, mostly in the language of math-
ematics; the environmentalist will build a draft with many
descriptive details; the historian will make good use of authoritative reports; the social caseworker may have a great
deal of anecdotal evidence. In every case, however, the most
effective pieces of writing will be constructed with specific
information.

Suggestion

Check your draft to see if there are basic forms of information that would make the draft stronger that you have not
used.

Where Do You Find Information?

One of the reasons I am glad to be a writer is that I am forced to
continue to learn. I have to mine my world for the specifics I
can use to discover what I have to say. The process of writing is
a process of thinking, but if the thinking is to be effective—and
if readers are going to read and use it—it must be built from
information. And to get that information I have to study my
subject.

Memory

We fear that writing will prove us ignorant. That has often happened in school when we were tested in writing. But, for writers, writing can show us how much we know. Your draft should have revealed your knowledge to you.

A writer's memory is an unusual gadget. I don't have a good memory in the TV game-show sense, but when I write about something, information arrives on my page that I have forgotten I knew or that I never knew I knew. My brain has recorded the details of the moment when I saw my first dead soldier in combat generations ago or that wonderful, awful evening when I looked down on my father for the first time and told him that if he hit me again, I'd belt him back. The same thing happens when I write on less personal topics. Ideas, quotations, statistics, references connect on the page.

If your draft did not show you how much you knew, you may need to take a step back and discover what you know that you didn't know you knew.

Before Writing
I start collecting information by brainstorming a list, putting down everything I know about the topic I am going to research. Or I fastwrite a "what-I-know" draft to surprise myself.

During Writing
While I am writing the draft I encourage the connections I do not expect, or make notes in the draft or on a pad of paper beside my computer of things I suddenly discover in the writing, references to other writing, connections between facts or ideas, new patterns of meaning, sources I have to explore.

Observation

In the academic world observation is often overlooked, yet it can be a productive source of significant information. If you are writing a paper on criminology, visit a police station or a jail; on health care, spend a few hours sitting in a hospital waiting room; on economics, walk through a supermarket or a mall; on literary studies, browse through that part of the library in which your subject is preserved; on government, attend a meeting of the school committee, town or city council.

When you observe, make notes. That activity will make you see more carefully as well as preserve what you observe. Note your first impression of a place, a book, a person. Make notes on what is and what is not; what is as you expected and what is not. Look for revealing details: how people interact (does the doctor listen to the patient?); where things are placed (are there forty-seven books about a man writer, two about a woman writer of the same period?), what is happening (are the trees thinner, have fewer leaves and branches because of acid rain?).

Use all your senses: sight, hearing, smell, taste, touch. Take account of how you feel, react. Imagine yourself in the prison cell, as a critic seeing a hundred-year-old work when it was first published, as the patient being examined.

Interview

Live sources should not be overlooked. If you are writing about schools, interview students present and past as well as teachers, administrators, school board members, parents. Read the books and articles about schools, but also go to see the people in the classrooms.

Many of the best interviewers are shy. The aggressive, on-the-scene journalist with microphone in the victim's face is *not* the best model for interviewing: "Did you have indigestion after you ate your twins?"

Good interviewers are good listeners. Few of us can turn away from a quiet, receptive listener who makes us an authority by asking our opinions. Try not to ask questions that can be answered with a simple "yes" or "no." Not, "Will you vote to make professors sing all their lectures?" but, "Why do you think it is important that professors sing their lectures?"

I like to prepare for an interview by listing the questions the reader will ask—and expect to have answered. There are usually five questions—give or take one—that must be answered if the reader is to be satisfied.

"Why is tuition being doubled?"
"How will the money be spent?"

"How do you expect it to affect students?"
"Why is it necessary to increase tuition?"
"What are you doing to help students who cannot pay?"

Listen to the questions and follow up on the answers to your questions: "We are raising tuition because the faculty is underpaid." "What evidence do you have that the faculty is underpaid? Can you name faculty members who have left because of pay? What positions are unfilled because the pay is so low?"

Note the answers to your questions, but check the ones you have any hesitation about or the ones that are most dramatic and surprising: "We are raising tuition so we can build the first-class ping-pong stadium our students demand." Journalists rarely check back with the person they interviewed, but I usually did. The purpose of the interview is not to trick the person being interviewed but to get accurate information to deliver to the reader.

Library

We live in an increasingly complex world. The Hong Kong stock exchange predicts Wall Street, a volcano in Alaska affects airlines in the lower forty-eight, a scientific breakthrough in Switzerland has immediate repercussions in Japan, politics in China sends shock waves around the world, a company in Des Moines is owned by a corporation in Dusseldorf and funded by loans from Tokyo. We are, indeed, a global village and in the center of that village is the library.

We need information on toxic wastes, traditions in Italian politics, arctic-survival techniques tested in Siberia and Canada, Norwegian exchange rates, the development of a new strain of AIDS virus in Africa and a treatment development in Paris, the translation of the work of a Nobel prizewinner who writes in Arabic—the list goes on and on. Libraries are the intellectual closets of humankind where information is stored until we need it.

Search Techniques
But can we find the information? Not in my closet, I find myself answering. Fortunately, humankind has bred librarians who

organize information so that it can be recovered. If I had written this book a few years ago I would have gone into great detail about the card catalogue and the Dewey Decimal System by which books have been catalogued, but the computer is changing—and greatly expanding—the way in which we recover information. Our library still has a card catalogue but only old fuds like me use it and new acquisitions are not entered in it. Most go to the line of computer terminals along the wall, and so will I because it has access to more information, and I can get a printout in many cases.

Your library will be changing and increasing its access to sources of information. Go to the reference desk, but do not only ask librarians at the desk to help you get information on your topic; instead, ask for instruction in how to use the library so that you can do your own research. That is a skill you'll need as a lawyer, salesperson, police officer, politician, social worker, doctor, scientist, teacher, nurse, retail-store manager. My auto dealer in rural New Hampshire has just had to install a satellite dish on his roof so he can be in instant touch with Jeep headquarters and their libraries of information, and through them to Peugeot headquarters in France.

I have a modem in my computer and through it I can use the library at the *Boston Globe.* I could plug into the University of New Hampshire library and I could subscribe to many services that would supply me with more information than I could handle at the stroke of a computer key.

The starting point for all the resources available to you—books, reference guides, monographs, articles, reports, audio and video tapes—is your librarian. Use the librarian to learn how you can tap into the abundance of information you need to draw on to write—and think—effectively.

Creating the Bibliography

The inexperienced library researcher pounces on an enticing piece of information and forgets to note where it came from. It is useless. It is no longer a piece of important information if it cannot be cited with an accurate attribution, if it cannot be checked by you and a reader.

Use a system of file cards, usually organized by topic and within that alphabetically by author, to record the complete title of your source, the author, the publisher, the copyright or publication date, the edition, the library reference number, the page on which you found the reference. Take down all the information that you or a reader may need and record that information in the way demanded by your discipline or in a way that will best serve anyone trying to find and use that reference.

It may be hard for those who have not used scholarly materials to understand the necessity of footnotes and bibliographies. It is not just to establish the authority of the writer but to serve the reader who is doing research, to let that interested reader follow the trail of scholarship that led to the writing. It is more than just etiquette; footnote references and bibliography are your duty if you are to participate in the intellectual world, adding your knowledge to those that went before you so that it is possible for those who come after you to build on your contributions.

Effective Note Taking

It is important to have a system of note taking so that you have accurate, readable (you ought to see *my* handwriting) notes with the source clearly indicated.

File Cards

Most writers find that the most efficient system involves note cards—three inches by five, four by six, or five by eight—on which most information can be placed, one to a card, together with the source. The cards can be carried easily to the library and ordered and reordered into categories as the research develops. It is easy to check back with cards and to line them up for reference while rewriting. (I think it is important to write the first draft without reference to the cards. That increases the flow of the text and what you remember is usually what you should remember; what you forget is what you should forget. But after the draft is done, you should check each fact, name, citation, quotation, statistic against the appropriate file card.)

Computer Notes

More and more people are typing their notes into a computer. This doesn't take the place of the original note cards but there are many software programs that do a spectacular job of organizing, ordering, and reordering information.

Print Out, Photo Copy, Fax

The electronic world in which we live has changed the way in which we collect and take notes. I do a great deal of photocopying when I research, making sure, however, that I write on each photocopied page where it came from. I either place these notes in a file folder—with the same heading as my computer file—or copy them into the computer. I also get printouts from computers or have a direct computer transfer of information into my computer files. Those are either placed in the stationary file or the computer file. Other material comes in by Fax and I treat it the same way. It is vital that you know where information comes from at every stage of the research and writing process.

Plagiarism

Plagiarism is using someone else's writing as if it were your own. I think it is a crime as serious as car theft or breaking and entering someone's home. I also know that many students do not know the difference between a quote and a paraphrase. A *quote* is using someone else's exact words.

> President Franklin D. Roosevelt said in his 1933 inaugural address during the heart of the Depression, "Let me assert my firm belief that the only thing we have to fear is fear itself—that nameless, unreasoning, unjustified terror which paralyzes needed efforts to convert retreat into advance."

The quoted words are enclosed in quotation marks (" ") and they are attributed to the person who said them by a direct attribution in the text, a footnote, or both. A *paraphrase* is putting someone else's idea in your own words.

> President Roosevelt told the nation that its fear of an economic disaster was more serious than the economic problems themselves.

Attribution

The reader deserves to know the source of the information. The reader ought to be skeptical, questioning the text, challenging its authority. And we have the obligation to answer that challenge.

Unstated

All the information in the text has an attribution. Information that has no footnote or reference is attributed to the writer. We must remember that and make the information we use on our own authority accurate, specific, and fair. We have personal responsibility for all we say in the text and we must say it in such a way that the reader trusts us.

Stated

In formal, academic research or scholarly writing, the attribution is provided by clear statements in the text together with a footnote, or with a footnote alone. The footnote style may vary in history, psychology, physics, zoology, mechanical engineering courses. Make sure you know the style each of your instructors expects.

You should remember, however, that in less formal writing, it is still important to provide, in the text itself, a reference: "As President George Bush said in his televised report to the nation on the action in Panama, December 20, 1989 . . . ." This will allow the reader to look up the original text.

Reader Granted Attribution

There is a third form of attribution, the one granted by the reader. When you write to a particular audience—police chiefs, supermarket managers, colonial historians, college undergraduates, town managers—you can refer to common experiences, express common opinions or frustrations, articulate the thoughts and feelings of your audience, and if they recognize and agree with what you are saying, that act grants you authority.

You may not have to attribute common knowledge—the Red Sox are having another losing season, New Hampshire has no broad-based sales or income tax—but you should indicate the source of any surprising or unusual information. This is a gray area and I would bend over backwards to make sure your reader knows the source of information central to a piece of writing that depends on research.

The best way to protect yourself is by being careful when you take notes. Use quotation marks around direct quotes, no quotation marks around a paraphrase, but be sure to identify the source of both. These are not your words or your ideas and the person to whom they belong deserves credit.

Suggestion

List the sources you can contact within the limits of time and geography who might have the information you need to support the meaning of your draft with accurate, specific information. Contact them and acquire the information you need.

Writing Information

Once the writer's information inventory is full, the challenge is to use selected information gracefully and effectively.

The Craft of Selection

Writing—and every other art—involves the craft of selection. The danger of collecting the necessary abundance of specific information is that the writer will attempt to include it all. An excess of information can clog the prose and obscure the message.

The reason for abundance is to allow the writer to choose the specific that reveals, the detail that clarifies, the fact that emphasizes, the fragment that provides authority, the information that moves the reader toward caring understanding.

A great deal of good material, information the writer worked hard to collect, will be left out. That is the mark of a good piece of writing. And, in a sense, it is all there anyway. The reader feels the abundance of information behind the page. The draft is not thin, it has depth and weight, it is worthy of attention.

Style

The style you will use to write with information will depend on the message you have to convey, the reader to whom you are writing, the occasion of writing, or the publication in which you are to appear, the genre in which your message is carried, the voice of the draft, but there are some basic techniques to consider.

Word

The individual word carries information to the reader, and to write lively, information-laden prose we should make sure that each word carries an adequate load of information to the reader. The words that can carry the most information are nouns and verbs.

Each case depends on the situation but consider the information contained in the simple words *house* and *home*—there's a choice worthy of consideration. Carry it further:

> **She lived in a** house.
> home.
> shack.
> mansion.
> hovel.
> palace.
> tenement.
> prefab.
> trailer.

And look at a simple, active verb:

> **He** walks **into the house.**
> slams
> strolls
> darts
> charges
> saunters
> dances
> tiptoes
> marches
> clumps

And the list can go on. And notice how much information a noun and a verb can convey in a simple sentence:

They	walked	**into the**	house.
	slammed		home.
	strolled		shack.
	darted		mansion.
	charged		hovel.
	sauntered		palace.
	danced		tenement.
	marched		prefab.
	clumped		trailer.

Now connect different nouns and verbs. Notice how you change the information and the message.

Phrase

The phrase, that fragment of language that is less than a sentence, is often an effective way to communicate information.

He walked the streets	like a soldier on patrol.*
	in fear of each shadow.
	as if he owned them.
	listening to his own footsteps.
	seeking the safety of shadows.
	unaware of who was following him.

Sentence

The simple sentence, as we have seen, can carry more information than we might expect, but we can load up the sentence with a great deal of information:

A university has been described, by Grayson Kirk, as a collection of colleges with a common parking problem, but I am struck, after returning to the university I attended, at how resilient an institution it is, welcoming unexpected thousands of veterans on the G. I. Bill after World War II and changing its curriculum, year after year, in response to society's need for study and research in many fields unheard of when I was

---

* (Now I'm in the game of writing: Can I say the same thing by simply changing *walked* to *patrolled?*)

an undergraduate: computer studies, space sciences, women studies and black studies, environmental sciences.

Paragraph

I think of paragraphs as the trailer trucks of prose that carry a heavy load of information to the reader:

> I wonder if my post-World War II generation will be known as the generation of the single-family house. I dreamt of living in a single-family home as I was brought up in rented flats where I was shushed by the fear that the neighbors upstairs or down might hear. Hear what? Anything. Music, fights, kitchen clatter, the Red Sox game, bed springs, bathroom flushes, burps, curses, footsteps, doors shutting, drawers opening. And then an uncle bought a single-family home in East Milton and I knew that was what I wanted. A house of my own, far enough from the neighbors to thump a ball, yell back, play my music at proper volume, flush the john after midnight. And I made it, one of the veterans who gloried in urban, suburban, and exurban sprawl. But my daughters, both successful, making more money than I did at their age, may never be able to afford a single-family home.

There are many other ways to carry information to the reader including illustration and graphics, but most information is communicated by word, phrase, sentence, and paragraph.

Remember that the reader is hungry for information. That is the principal reason we have readers. They want to read the specific, accurate, interesting information that will turn them into authorities on our subjects.

Suggestion

Go through your draft and make the information specific and accurate in fact and context. Change a word with a general meaning such as *beautiful* to a specific example, like *the flight of a seagull,* which creates a vivid image. Use precise statistics, direct quotations, sharp images, proper nouns that do not need adjectives, active verbs that do not depend on adverbs for clear meaning. You will see the text become lively and authoritative under your hand.

= 8 =

Revise for Voice

Now the fun begins.

I have discovered meaning; I have read my readers and discovered their needs; I have ordered my draft; I have selected convincing evidence; I have created a draft that is ready for line-by-line editing. I am ready to work with language, to tune the voice of the text, to practice the final stage of the writer's craft.

Fine-tuning with language is satisfying play. I find a more specific word and fit it into place, I hear the beat of music rising from within the draft and make it clear to the reader, I slow down the draft or speed it up, I wrench a sentence from a tangle of clauses and allow it to run free, I move information in the paragraph so its importance is revealed, I put in a "spontaneous" touch or two, I read and rewrite and reread and rewrite again and again until the draft is ready to leave me and find its own readers.

Hearing Your Voice

Listening, that is what the writer does during this process of reading and writing. The writer writes with the ear, hearing what is on the page and what is not yet on the page: The tune of meaning is often heard, then played. The writer listens for the writer's own voice, then tunes it to the draft so that the human music of voice supports and advances meaning.

What Do You Mean by Voice?

Voice is the magic quality in writing. Voice is what allows the reader's eyes to move over silent print and *hear* the writer speaking. Voice is the quality in writing, more than any other, that makes the reader read on, that makes the reader interested in what is being said and makes the reader trust the person who is saying it. We return to the columns, articles, poems, books we like because of the writer's individual voice. Voice is the music in language.

Many of the qualities writers call voice have been called style in the past, but writers today generally reject that term. Style seems to be something that can be bought off the rack, something that can be imitated easily. *Tone* is another word that is used but this seems limited to one aspect of writing. *Voice* is a more human term, and one with which we are familiar.

We all know—and make use of—the individual quality of voice. We recognize the voice of each member of our family from another room; we recognize the voices of our friends down the dormitory corridor or across the dining hall. And we know that voice isn't just the sound of the voice, it is the way each person says things. We enjoy Anne's stories; Kevin's quick rejoinders; the fascinating details Andrea calls attention to; Mark's quiet, straight-faced humor; Tori's mock anger; Reggie's genuine rage.

Their voices reflect the way they see the world, how they think, how they feel, how they make us pay attention to the world they see. And we are used to using our own voices, plural intended, to tell others our concerns, our demands, our needs.

My daughters learned to use their voices with Machiavellian skill while still in the crib; and most of us are virtuosos of the rage, real and mock; the whine; the demand; the plead; the voices of seduction, acceptance, rejection; the office voice and the school voice and the home voice; the street voice and the family voice; the voices of humor and irony and skepticism and belief and disbelief and love. Continue the list. You are all manipulators of the spoken voice and well prepared to consider voice in writing.

When we write we should write out loud, hearing what we say as—or just before—we say it. The magic of writing is that the words on the page are heard by the reader. Individual writer *speaks* to individual reader. The heard quality of speech is put into writing by the experienced writer.

Voice also has a political element. Voice speaks out; voice demands to be heard. The person who has voice is empowered. A person whose voice can be heard in writing has an opportunity to influence the policies of a government, a school, an agency, a corporation, a society. Voices that demand listening may attract hearers who may add their voices to the cause. Information is power and voice gives information focus and significance.

I am a writer because I am selfish, the infant screaming from the crib. I want to be heard. I am a teacher of writing because I want others to be heard, those who are black, brown, yellow, and pale; those who are poor, almost poor, and rich; those who are young and old; the outs and the ins; the empowered and the powerless; the comforted and the discomforted; the angry and the content; the risk takers and the safe players all raising their voices in a glorious cacophony from which we all learn.

Hearing All Your Voices

Voice is often seen as a mystery, an element in writing that is sophisticated, difficult for the student to understand. Baloney. I have never had a student who did not come to the first class knowing—and using—many voices.

Before going to first grade, children know there are voices they use in playing they may not use in church, ways of speaking that are not appropriate in front of grandmother, voices that will win permission from one parent and not another, voices that will make peers come over to play or run away home. We all speak before language, when we cry from the crib, with many voices.

The Personal Voice
We start with our personal voices, as individual as our finger-prints. Can you tell who is speaking in the next room at home? Of course. That is Mother's voice or Dad's, Jim's or Ruth's, Aunt Irma's, the social worker's, or the police officer's.

Ethnic Influences
We are the product of our racial heritage. There is such a thing as Jewish humor or Black humor—which may not be black humor. Sorry, that may be an example of Scottish humor. On my first visit to Scotland I looked up a relative and found an old man digging in a garden. "Are you Donald Bell?" I asked. "Guilty as charged," he answered. I had thought that was a family joke in America and found it was Scottish humor that emigrated to America. It was not a family retort but a typically Scottish retort. My voice—and yours—is a product of heritage, all those elements that arrive in your genes.

Regional Influences
Our voices are also the product of the speaking habits of the area in which we are brought up. My speech is urban not country, street language not field language; I speak fast and say "Cuber" for Cuba and "Hahvud Squah" for Harvard Square; I speak Boston—perhaps the ugliest accent in America—not Boston Brahmin but Boston working class. Our ears pick up the patterns of speech around us and we make them our own.

Family Influences
Each family has its way of speaking and we learn speech by imitation. No wonder, that for the rest of our lives, we hear the ghosts of those family members who are dead or live far away, in our spoken and written voices. When my oldest daughter makes a list, and she makes many because she inherited that compulsion from me, I see my handwriting in her handwriting, and I hear traces of my wife's Kentucky family in phrases she and her sister-in-law use.

Daily Influences
We all swim in a sea of language.

Peers   Those we hang out with invade our voices with their own words, phrases, sentences, with their rhythm and pacing. We want to belong and perhaps the clearest sign of belonging is in our speech. We don't want to speak funny, we want to conform—in dress, gesture, walk, attitude—and speech.

School   Each class in school, each school corridor, cafeteria, gymnasium, playground is a language laboratory. We can often be identified as jock, brain, nerd, geek by how we speak. Many of us, of course, belong to several groups and we change our speech chameleon-like when we go from field-hockey locker room to library.

Church and Work   There are many institutional influences in our lives. I attended a million, it seemed, evangelical sermons when I was young and at times I can spot that music in my writing. My writing style is often journalistic—direct sentences, short paragraphs, active voice—because I worked and work in that linguistic environment. When you say "perpetrator" I suspect you have been a police officer as I have, when you say "user friendly" I imagine you share my familiarity with computers.

Reading, TV, and Radio   To write more effectively, read. Our language is rich with the written voices of the past and present. Do not cheat yourself of either. As writers, we need to know how the masters of the past, in English and in all the great languages of the world, used their voices; we also need to hear the voices of our own generation in essay and poem, article and history, stage play and screenplay, biography and autobiography, short story and novel, from each of the cultures that enrich our lives—African and Oriental, European and South American and North American.

And we need to be careful of the influence of radio and TV. The programs broadcast on these powerful media are written, but not many are written well. I notice the writing in "LA Law" and "In the Heat of the Night." When you are impressed by a drama, a comedy series, a commentator, you should realize that it is the product of a carefully crafted writing. But in an age of pollution, we suffer language pollution and most of it comes from radio and TV where the cliché—the worn-out, meaningless phrase—reigns.

Your Language or Mine?

School's view of language often seems authoritative, a matter of rules, as if language were stopped at this moment, a matter of clear right and wrong. School doesn't really mean that. The history of language is the history of change but school has the responsibility to communicate the traditions of the moment, to help students know how language is currently used so people can communicate with each other.

This inevitably gets mixed up with status and etiquette. The "educated" person speaks differently from the "uneducated" one; the person in power uses language differently from the person out of power; the well-mannered person speaks differently from the uncouth, uncultured one.

I am uncomfortable with those ideas but they have a truth. I do not come from a well-educated family. They did pay a great deal of attention to speaking properly but my education isolated me from my background and my family. I recognize the need of people to learn the language of those who have power over them but I also respect the languages and dialects of all the diverse cultures in our society. The grandmother who brought me up spoke Gaelic but she would not teach a word of it to me. I was to be an "American" and to speak "American." Sadly I became monolingual and was cheated of the heritage of Gaelic literature, oral and written, with which I should have been familiar.

I am writing a textbook of revision and inevitably I seem to say, "Write like me" and that makes me uncomfortable. And yet, the world judges you, more than it should, by how you speak and write. If you want to be heard, to be empowered, you have to find your way to use our language, not your own, and eventually to enrich our language with your own.

The Importance of Your Voice

Voice is the most important element in writing. It is what attracts, holds, and persuades your readers.

Significance
Voice illuminates information. Voice makes what appears to be insignificant information significant, and an ineffective voice can make what is significant for readers appear to be insignificant.

Your voice delivers meaning to the reader. That meaning may not be simple, but it must be clear. Everything expressed by the writer's voice—the pauses between words, the pace of the words, the specific pieces of information, the beat and sound of language—must advance and clarify your meaning.

Character

Voice is a matter of character. The reader may think the writer can conceal with words and rhetoric; politicians and corporations try but they are exposed to the critical reader. I have free-lanced as a corporate and Cabinet ghostwriter and know that my words would reveal better than conceal. When the corporation lost money, we said that up front, together with why and what we intended to do about it. We did not lie because we could not. As an editorial writer I was never asked to write an opinion in which I did not believe. It would show.

Trust

An effective voice demonstrates that it is an authority on the subject. It speaks with confidence in specific terms. It is sure enough to qualify, to admit problems, to allow weaknesses of argument; it does not shout and bang the desk but speaks quietly to the individual reader, for writing is a private act—one writer to one reader. The writer's voice endeavors to earn the trust of the reader.

Music

Language is music. Writing is heard as it is read. The effective voice is tuned to the message, the situation, and the reader. The music of the writer's voice, similar to the music accompanying the movie, supports and advances the meaning of the entire text.

Communication

The effective voice can be heard, respected, and understood by a reader. Writing is a public act performed in private and received in private. Both reader and writer are alone. The writer must anticipate the language of the reader so that the act of writing will be completed when the writer's message is absorbed by the reader.

The Expected Voice

Society expects certain voices from us according to the message we have to deliver and the place it will be delivered. The voice of the victorious locker room is different from the losing one; the funeral voice different from the party voice. When we read science fiction, a newspaper sports story, a war report in a magazine, an economics—or composition—textbook, we have expectations.

The effective writer knows what the reader expects and decides to write within or against those expectations. But if the writer works against the expectations—using a poem to report on a football game, a narrative as a corporation's annual report—the reader must be informed in some way that the writer is aware of going against expectations. The reader must be prepared because the expectations of the reader are always strong.

The Reasons for Tradition

We need expectations—traditions—in language. Without the traditions of language there would be no communication, just a babel of sounds. And the traditions need to be shared. When I was overseas in England during World War II, British women, when asked for a date, would say, "Knock me up at seven," not realizing they were issuing a startling command to the shocked soldier who thought that he spoke the same language. And by using that example I am working against the expectation of a textbook voice.

How to Use Tradition

We learn the traditions of our language better by osmosis than by rule, by reading and listening, by writing to see what is understood and what is not. Few of us learn efficiently from studying rules for an act we are not performing, the book on how to kiss is understood best by those who have had the impulse to kiss and acted upon it. Write, then study the rules in the context of using written language to communicate meaning.

The Formal Voice

In school and at work, we learn the traditions of the formal voice, the literary research paper, the lab report, the nursing notation, the business memo. These formal traditions are usually rigid for good reason. The doctor scanning the nurse's night-time notations is not looking for an aesthetic experience or a philosophical essay on pain, but clear, specific information to help modify treatment.

Footnotes and bibliographies are designed to serve the scholarly readers of scholarly publications; professional language required of an accounting or engineering report conveys specific information with the requisite precision. We must read, study, and learn the traditions of each field in which we intend to publish.

The Informal Voice

What we may not understand is that the informal voice has its own traditions. When we write a thank-you note to Aunt Agatha, a humor column in a college newspaper, a note stuck on a door to tell a roommate where we are eating, we also follow traditions. The style may be casual, but it is usually in a casual tradition. Jeans and sneaks may be just as traditional as gown and high heels. We need to know the tradition, then try to vary it if the tradition interferes with the delivery of our message.

Genre Voices

Each genre has its own way of using language. In school we learn the academic voices of those disciplines we study. The formalities of the literature paper may be quite different from those of the paper in economics, education, botany, business administration, history. Ask the professor in the course for the style manual of that profession. Make sure you know the form and the language each professor expects.

Narrative, journalism, drama, poetry, biography, and autobiography all have their own traditions that you can discover by asking people in each field to tell you its tradition, where it is published, or by reading in that form. There are many languages of lyric poetry or of jazz, folk, or rock lyrics, but each belongs to a tradition that can be defined and described.

When To Ignore Tradition

George Orwell, whose essays are among the most respected in English, once published these rules:

(i)   Never use a metaphor, simile or other figure of speech which you are used to seeing in print.

(ii)   Never use a long word where a short one will do.

(iii) If it is possible to cut a word out, always cut it out.

(iv) Never use the passive where you can use the active.

(v)   Never use a foreign phrase, a scientific word or jargon word if you can think of an everyday English equivalent.

(vi) Break any of these rules sooner than say anything barbarous.

These are marvelous rules that I have posted in my writing rooms from time to time; the most important one is:

Break any of these rules sooner than say anything barbarous.

Break any rule that causes you to say what is not true, that makes language awkward, that impedes communication, that creates a sour note in the music of your text.

The Text's Voice

Traditional education focuses on—surprise—the traditional voice; untraditional education focuses on the personal voice. I think they both miss the target. We need to know how to use the conventions of traditional language, and we need to be able to hear the sound of our personal voice, but the focus should be on the voice of the individual text. Voice, as we have said, is a matter of situation; what is appropriate for one message, in one genre, for one reader, may not be in another.

Listen to the Voice of the Text

We need to train ourselves to listen to the voice that emerges from the draft, we need to hear how language is being used in this particular case. Of course what we will hear will be a blend of personal and traditional voices woven together for this particular purpose. That should provide the focus: What is needed here? What is strong and right? What needs to be extended and developed?

We have to be able to work at the console of language mixing the tracks we hear so they work together to produce a combined voice—the voice of the text—that will communicate our meaning.

> ### Suggestion
>
> Choose a personal experience that has affected your life and take ten minutes to describe it in writing. If you work on a computer, turn the screen off; if not, try not to pay attention to how your draft looks. Speak the draft out loud, hear what you are saying as you are saying it, follow the beat, the rhythm, the tone, the melody of what you are saying. Stop after ten minutes and read your draft aloud to hear your voice arise from the page.

Tuning the Voice of the Draft

After you have heard your own voice, you are ready to adapt it to the needs of the text you are producing, tuning your natural way of speaking to the demands of the message and the needs of the reader.

The Attitude of the Revising Writer

Educational jargon: The affective controls the cognitive. Rewritten in understandable terms: How you feel determines how you will think. Try again: The attitude you bring to a task determines how you will perform the task. Tie to rewriting: The attitude you bring to revision determines how well you will revise. Qualify it? Oh, well: The attitude you bring to revision *often* determines how well you will revise.

It is a waste of time to discuss skills before we discuss the attitudes of the craftsperson using those skills. I love to revise and that, in itself, is an attitude I've developed. I used to hate to rewrite but my attitude changed with the experience of rewriting; I learned to be comfortable with revision, saw how it improved my drafts, began to enjoy it. Here are some of the attitudes I bring to the writing desk.

Writing Is Rewriting

It is not admission of failure when you have to rewrite and edit. It is a normal part of the process of making meaning with language. Revision is not punishment, but an opportunity.

You Are the Reader's Advocate

When you revise, you become the reader's advocate. You step back, drop the natural possessiveness we all have about what we have written, and read as a stranger. To get distance on my own copy I often have to name the stranger—an intelligent friend who doesn't care about my subject. He or she will read with disinterest and without familiarity or concern. That's just the reader I want to reach, and so I read my draft through their eyes.

My Ear Revises Better than My Hand

We spoke before we wrote, historically and individually. Writing is not quite speech written down but it is speech transformed so that it may be heard. The voice lies silent within the page, ready to be turned on by a reader.

We know our language best by hearing it and speaking it. Writing is an oral/aural act and we do well to edit out loud, hearing the text as we revise and polish it. Should we add this, slow that down, speed it up here, take time to define this term, use this word, this construction? What is traditional and expected by the reader? What best supports and communicates the meaning of the draft? These questions can often be answered by reading the line out loud, taking something out and reading it out loud, putting something in and reading it out loud. Hand, eye, and *ear*, a constant interplay.

My Draft Will Tell You What It Needs

I have learned to respect my draft. Writing is not an ignorant act. Something was happening when the draft was being written. Writers know the contradiction of art: There is usually reason in accident. Try to understand the text on its own terms. Do not make it what you or the world expects, but what the text itself commands.

Welcome Surprise

I still learn during revision. The draft—the act of making a draft—teaches me what I know and need to know about a subject—and its writing.

Language Is Alive and Changing

This writer sees language as ever changing. I may not like all the changes—I growl at split infinitives and grump when people use *host* as a verb even if it is now listed as a verb in dictionaries—but most of the time I delight in our changing language and work as a writer at the edge of tradition. That is where the writer is using language to say what has not quite been said before in a way that has not quite been heard before.

Language is not a simple matter of right or wrong but a complex matter of music and meaning. The purpose of language is to make clear, and what needs to be made clear may not be simple at all. The writer uses voice to articulate the thoughts and feelings that readers discover are their own.

To do this the writer must know tradition but also extend it, trying what cannot yet be done, seeking new combinations of words, even new made-up words, new language music, new patterns of line, sentence, and paragraph. The writer works with tradition, or the reader will not understand, and against tradition so that what hasn't been said may be said, and the language will grow from the writer's experiments.

The writer's guide is not right or wrong but what works and what doesn't. No decision about language can be made in the abstract any more than a surgeon should decide to operate without seeing the patient. All editing decisions are context oriented; what may be correct in one place may not be in another. Writing's job is not to be correct but to communicate meaning.

The writer employs language to produce a written voice that will be heard and understood by the reader.

Accept Limitations

I accept the limitations of my craft—the assigned length of the draft, the expected form and tone, the targeted reader, the deadline—then go beyond the acceptance to view the limitations as a creative challenge. The mural is different from the miniature, the song from the opera, the jazz combo from the big band. The limitations of any art contribute to its breakthroughs; it is not discipline or freedom alone that is at the center of craft but the tension between freedom and discipline.

Establish Achievable Standards

Student writers and professional writers, myself certainly included, tend to dream an impossible draft. That is a certain route to failure. We give up before beginning the draft, knowing we can't do it; we quit while drafting because we are not living up to an imaginary standard; we toss the final draft because it doesn't measure up to an unreasonable standard.

The Feel of Line-by-Line Revising

The feel of practicing a craft is first cousin to attitude yet most books never discuss the feel of writing and rewriting, the experience of feeling a draft grow under your hand, eye, ear.

Revision is an intimate involvement with the emerging final draft. Way back there was the blank page and the hint of what might appear on that page; now there is a draft and actual language that can be cut and developed and moved about, shaped and adapted to your evolving meaning. It is a physical matter now, nothing vague and abstract, not a matter of theory and principle, but the gardener digging and planting and weeding, the baker mixing then kneading the dough, the player reacting to a fake then cutting toward the basket.

Seamus Heaney has written a poem that captures the feeling I have when revising:

Digging
Between my finger and my thumb
The squat pen rests; snug as a gun.

Under my window, a clean rasping sound
When the spade sinks into gravelly ground;
My father, digging. I look down

Till his straining rump among the flowerbeds
Bends low, comes up twenty years away
Stooping in rhythm through potato drills
Where he was digging.

The coarse boot nestled on the lug, the shaft
Against the inside knee was levered firmly.
He rooted out tall tops, buried the bright edge deep
To scatter new potatoes that we picked
Loving their cool hardness in our hands.

By God, the old man could handle a spade.
Just like his old man.

My grandfather cut more turf in a day
Than any other man on Toner's bog.
Once I carried him milk in a bottle
Corked sloppily with paper. He straightened up
To drink it, then fell to right away

Nicking and slicing neatly, heaving sods
Over his shoulder, going down and down
For the good turf. Digging.

The cold smell of potato mould, the squelch and slap
Of soggy peat, the curt cuts of an edge
Through living roots awaken in my head.
But I've no spade to follow men like them.

Between my finger and my thumb
The squat pen rests.
I'll dig with it.

Editing is a physical act. The writer enters the text and
starts rearranging the furniture. You move in close with pencil,
pen, or cursor on the screen, looking at the word, hearing the
word, trying another word, seeing its effect on the words that
follow, discarding it, trying another, reading the word, reading
the line, scanning the paragraph, fitting, choosing, trying;
shaping and polishing; moving in close, then standing back;
reading as the maker then reading as a stranger.

This is always exciting for me. I see, as the photographer
sees in the darkroom, the meaning coming clear under my
hand. I am discovering—in detail—the meaning toward which
I have been moving in the earlier drafts.

And now I experience the satisfactions of craft. There are
few things as much fun as the unexpected touch of humor, the
surprising insight, the delight of the right word, the sentence

running free on its own purpose, the filled-out and shaped paragraph.

Line-by-line I liberate the text, letting it go, as I let my daughters go, into its own life, where its meaning will change and develop as it is read.

The Craft of Revision

From Part to Whole—and Back

To revise effectively, the writer has to be an intellectual acrobat, leaping from the general to the particular and back, again and again and again while reading and writing the text. We can break down many of the activities performed simultaneously during the writing process but this sophisticated kind of reading depends on an interaction in which the parts cannot be separated.

Let's try, however, to look at the writer reading during revision to see if we can glimpse interactions that take only a fraction of a second.

I remember the intent with which the sentence was written: to re-create the experience of returning to the classroom after three years in the Army. Holding that intent in my mind, I read the specific words in the sentence: *I was alienated as I went to my first class.*

I misread it, hearing myself say "felt" instead of "was" and changed the sentence, realizing I was talking about feelings: *I felt alienated as I went to my first class.*

The particular word, *felt,* had affected my general intent or meaning. My mind had raced from meaning to word and back to meaning. And now my critical mind kicked in. The sentence seemed flat, meaningless, it asked the reader to make up the meaning of the word *alienated.* I decided to make my memory go to work and transport me back all those years. I did not think, then write. I am a writer and my way of thinking is writing. I plunged in and rewrote the sentence: *I felt angry as I went to my first class.*

I was surprised, and as a writer I welcome surprise. I thought about the word and remembered a deep, motivating anger that we carried home with us after the war and how different we saw that world than how it looks from the vantage point of history. The specific word *angry* had changed my evolving meaning. But what was I angry about? I wrote the sentence again, making it more immediate, more active to see if that would transport back over the years: *I feel the banked fire* [Will the young reader who has not tended a coal furnace understand this? Don't worry about it now. It is a metaphor of that time, that place, keep going] *of rage as I stand at the door of my first class after the war: The 4-Fs who didn't go to war had the jobs and I resented going back to school to see if I could make it into the middle class, live in a single-family house.*

Those specific words have developed my meaning. I am now writing about the resentment we felt against those who had stayed home and gotten "our" jobs.

We can only demonstrate a small part of the complex interactions within the brain when we write, but this example rings true to my experience, and I should add that I did not "know" this before I wrote it. I had not thought much about this aspect of my personal history but now, as a result of this interaction of the particular and the whole, I have a topic that I may explore in my next column for the *Boston Globe*.

The Tools of Revision

Beginning writers have too much respect for their written drafts. They have been taught to respect—or fear, or stand in awe of, or to admire without question—the printed text. The writing, especially if it is typed, appears finished.

The experienced writer likes nothing so much as despoiling a neatly printed text. The writer cuts right into the neatness, messing around. The writer cuts and adds and moves around and puts back what was just cut and discards and redrafts.

Now I write on a computer, where my best friend is the button marked "delete." I draft and revise while always having a neat, readable text on my screen. But for decades before the computer age I revised, and my office still has the tools I used—and occasionally still use—to make my final draft look easy, natural, even spontaneous.

My tools are a wastebasket, large; scissors; glue (stapler, scotch tape); a black, thick-line felt marker; an extra-fine black pen. I can discard, cut and paste, cross out, and insert.

Some of the ways the writer marks an evolving draft include:

Cross out	The ~~lazy~~ dog runs.
Take out	The ~~lazy~~ dog runs⌒slowly.
Put back in	The ~~lazy~~ dog runs slowly.
Transpose	The lazy dog⌢runs⌣slowly.
Insert	The lazy dog ~~runs slowly~~ saunters.
Move	(The lazy dog runs slowly.)
Period	The lazy dog runs⊙slowly.
Capital	The lazy dog runs. slowly.

The important thing is to mark the text so that you can see the changes and read the text as it will appear after the changes are made to see if more changes are necessary—and they usually are because the particular changes the meaning and the meaning influences the particular.

The Revision Check List

As we read during revision, moving back and forth from meaning to specific, we deal with a complex blend of overlapping concerns. It is helpful, especially in the beginning, to develop your own check list of the elements that contribute to voice. Eventually this may become instinctive but in writing this chapter I had to study my own revision practices to reverse this process and articulate my instinctive check list forged over decades of revision. In doing it, I surprised myself by some of the elements—the primary importance of specifics, "Is it me?," "Does it use tradition?," and their order. The "it" in the questions is awkward but it represents the genre of the draft or the particular section of the draft being revised, as I will demonstrate later. Here is my check list for tuning my voice:

Is it specific?
Is it true?
Is it me?

Does it fit?
Is it clear?
Will the reader read?
Does it advance the meaning?
Does it use tradition?
Does it flow?

Now let's take that list and examine the implications of each question.

Is It Specific?

I was surprised to discover this was my first concern. But I find it appropriate after reconsidering it. We write with information, not free floating language; words are the symbols for specific information. And the more specific the language, the more the reader believes and trusts the writer. Specific words also give off vibrations, multiplying their effect on the reader: *Dance* is a good noun and it may be the accurate one, but *prom* carries with it special emanations as does *ball*. Finally, specific language is lively, easy, and interesting to read.

Is It True?

Unfortunately, it is easy to lie with specifics, and I find myself hyping my own copy. I have to stop and make sure that everything—word for word—is accurate in itself and in the context of the line, the paragraph, the section, the entire work.

Is It Me?

It has taken me most of my sixty-five years to accept myself. I wanted to be old when I was young, young when I became old; heavy when I was a string bean, thin when I became a pear; to write like Toni Morrison, Mekeel McBride, A. E. Housman, E. B. White, Sharon Olds, George Orwell, Gustave Flaubert, Robert Caro, Christopher Scanlan, Wil Haygood, when I could only write like me. I have to tune my voice to my own way of making music on the page.

Does It Fit?

Nothing in writing stands by itself; we have to be master cabinet-makers who can fit everything together so that our final drafts contain their full load of meaning and stand up to a reader's scrutiny. The word has to fit the words before it and the ones that come next; the phrase has to fit the line; the line the paragraph; the paragraph the section; the section the whole piece.

Is It Clear?

When I am revising my draft, I try to practice George Orwell's rule: "Good writing is like a window pane." I do not want to call attention to myself but to my subject; I do not want to get between the reader and the subject. When I have problems making my writing clear, I find it helpful to concentrate on the word *reveal;* I try to reveal my subject to my reader or, better yet, to allow my subject to reveal itself to my reader.

Will the Reader Read?

I am my first reader and I have to make myself the attorney for all the readers that will follow. Is the information placed in a position that gives it proper emphasis; have I been as simple as possible without oversimplifying the subject; is the draft paced so that the reader is propelled forward but still allowed time to absorb each point before being moved on to the next one, have I asked the reader's questions—and answered them?

Does It Advance the Meaning?

Every piece of information, every word and the sound of every word, every comma and semi-colon, every sound, every space, should serve the meaning of the draft. No matter how interesting an anecdote you have, how dramatic a quote, how fascinating a fact, how clever a phrase, it should not survive revision if it does not advance the meaning of the draft in the reader's mind.

Does It Use Tradition?

The traditions of our written culture—rhetoric, grammar, mechanics, usage, spelling—are the record of the conventions that successful writers in the past and present have used to communicate meaning. They are not laws that must be followed—remember Orwell's sixth rule, "Break any of these rules sooner than say anything barbarous"—but they are traditions that have worked in the past and that the reader expects to be employed today. Conform to them when they help you communicate your meaning, as they will most of time, and go against expectation when they do not.

Does It Flow?
After all this fiddling around, cutting that, inserting this, moving the other stuff around, making changes in information and position, meaning and sound, the draft must be smoothed over so that none of the effort shows. The music of the final draft should flow with an easy naturalness so the reader is absorbed in what is said, not how the writer has said it.

Applying the Check List

Facing a draft can seem hopeless, but armed with the check list, there are really only four levels of concern when you tune the voice of your draft: the word, the line, the paragraph, the draft. And that is the sequence I follow.

- You revise the word, applying it to the evolving meaning of the draft.
- You return with that evolving meaning and revise the line, applying it to the evolving meaning of the draft.
- You return with that evolving meaning and revise the paragraph, applying it to the evolving meaning of the draft.
- You return with that revolving meaning and apply it to the entire draft.

Don't despair. It becomes a natural process and it is fun because you can see your meaning change and grow stronger, hear your voice grow more effective and graceful.

Revising the Word

The craft of writing—and the art—begins with the word that ignites the draft, and it ends with the word that will rise off the page and enter the reader's brain. Not any word, the right word. Mark Twain said it best: "The difference between the right word and the almost-right word is the difference between lightning and a lightning-bug."

The word is so important that most young writers become fascinated with words in themselves. They collect longer words, fancier words, strange words they have never heard before, words that make funny sounds, words that call attention to the writer instead of the meaning. They become word drunk, and some writers never sober up. However, most writers who are read recover from vocabularyism. They have learned through writing for readers that the word has no value in itself; the value of the word comes from the information it communicates. A check has no value if you can't cash it. A word has no value unless it communicates information, not the fancy word, not the word to impress, but the simple word that carries meaning directly and clearly to the reader's mind.

Apply the check list to the words in your draft.

Is the word specific?
Is the word true?
Is the word mine?
Does the word fit?
Is the word clear?
Will the reader read?
Does the word advance the meaning?
Does the word use tradition?
Does the word flow?

Notes for the Writer Revising the Word

I am going to take you inside the craft of revision with one writer—myself—and share the mental notes I keep in my mind as I revise the word.

Find the Right Word
The game of words is one of the most fascinating humans can play. We all know a simple word such as *walk*. But is it so simple? *Walk* means simply to put one foot in front of another, but when a vinyl-siding salesperson comes to the door and I say, "Take a walk," it means there's no sale potential here; when the union leader tells the boss, "We walk," it means the workers go on strike; and when the umpire says, "Walk," it means the batter gets to trot to first base. And think of all the walks there are: stroll, saunter, march, stride, shuffle, promenade, tiptoe, and on and on and on. My job is to find the right word, the single word that reflects the meaning I need to communicate.

There are a number of ways to check on the meaning of the word you have used to see if you have chosen the right word—the word that communicates meaning accurately and gracefully.

1. *Recall* all the meanings of the word to see if you have the right one. Most words have many meanings—*hit,* for example, can mean a blow to someone, an attempt at seduction, a gangland murder, a baseball activity, a popular song—and you should be sure you are using the one your reader will understand.

2. *Read aloud* to hear the meaning of the word. We are most experienced with spoken language, and we will hear a wrong word that we read right over silently.

3. *Consider the context* in which the word is being used. If I say, "I don't know no grammar," *no* is the wrong word but if I am demonstrating my ignorance, it may be the right word *in context.*

4. *Check the words* you marked in bold face, capital letters or underlining on the first draft so they stand out when you come to edit the final draft. While writing an early draft you will often use a word you knew was not right but you did not want to slow the flow of the writing to use the dictionary. Sometimes I will put a question mark in parentheses (?) or brackets [?] after the word or even bracket a note to myself: [cliche], [weak word—make stronger], [vague—make specific].

5. *Look up* the definitions of any word you do not use naturally in normal speech—and even some of those, if you are using them in an unusual way.

Use Simple Words

I am a writer fascinated with the power of simple words. I may have to use complex words if I am writing about a complex subject but I will still use the simplest word I can find.

Hear the Music of the Word

Each word performs its own music. *Zip* is different from *zap, maim* from *hurt, guffaw* from *giggle, mumble* from *grunt.* I want the music of each word—the musical note—to contribute to the music that supports and communicates the meaning of the draft.

Select the Reader's Word

If our language is different from our reader's language, then we exclude. I want to include. I do not want to write in formal, academic rhetoric, but neither can I speak undergraduate. It is a long time since I was an undergraduate, and if I try to use today's slang I'll miss or sound patronizing, so I try to write in a lively way that draws the reader in.

Define the Word

When I use a word that is unfamiliar to my audience—such as *lede*—I try to define it immediately—"lede, the newspaper term for the beginning sentences or paragraphs in a news story." I don't often need to use a footnote or a formal definition and I first try to define the word by the context in which it is used. "The news writer first concentrates on the beginning of the story, trying to get the lede right before going on."

Avoid Clichés

Clichés are worn-out expressions that belong in the dumpster: *couch potato, real cool, freaked out.* The first time I heard *couch potato* it brilliantly described a couple of guys one of my daughters had dated. I howled, but such expressions repeated on radio and TV, at the mall, dormitory party, in the living room, become meaningless. Once in a while you can play with them— "he was a sweet couch potato," "he was a couch pancake," "he was a beach potato"—but such tricks of the trade have a limited life as well.

Our first-draft writing is often full of clichés that were once, like the new TV commercial, amusing or insightful— perhaps both—but are worn out with use such as *couch potato:* trite, "so tired I could die"; stereotyped, "cross as a bear"; slang, "airhead"; all grown meaningless with overuse.

How do you recognize them? By their familiarity. Listen to the speech of your friends—we all have difficulty hearing our own. Notice how many times you know what people are going to say before they say it, notice how many times the same phrases are used—those are clichés. Cut them out, say what you mean by using your own eyes, ears, voice.

Resist Jargon

Every trade has its jargon—*software* may be an example of jargon that has made it into the language because it has a specific meaning—but most jargon is private language that excludes. It is used to demonstrate that you are a member of a club and the reader is not. Again, I want to include as many readers as possible in my writing.

And jargon gets sloppy, the same word means one thing to a clinical psychologist, quite another to an experimental psychologist. One of the problems for those of us who use different computer programs is that the jargon of one program is not consistent with another. Avoid jargon; write in clear terms.

Write with Verbs and Nouns
I always feel a bit guilty—not the full weight of *sin* but a little twinge of guilt—when I use an adverb or an adjective. I use them but it means that I have not found the right verb or noun, that I hope to catch the meaning between two words, and meaning is better caught with one word. At the most important points in my text I double my concentration on finding *the* verb, *the* noun.

Write in the Active Voice
When I was English Department chairperson and a faculty member was voted tenure, my note often went something like this: "You got it. Congratulations." When the opposite was true I was more likely to sound like this: "It was the opinion of the committee that, after consideration, it would seem appropriate that we would not grant tenure at this time." Passive, wordy, and a tone that avoided personal responsibility.

Avoid the passive voice. "John hit Jim" is far more direct— and 40 percent shorter—than "Jim was hit by John."

Watch Out for the Verb To Be
The verb *to be* in all its forms is a workhorse of our language but we can overwork it: "I will be seeing you outside" is pure clutter. "I'll see you outside" does the same job quicker and clearer. Make sure that the verb *to be* doesn't clutter up your draft.

Cut Unnecessary Words
Each word should carry its weight of meaning. This doesn't mean you write like a telegram, but it does mean that you check each word during revision. You may have stuck in such a clutter word as *however*. It may need to be cut, but it may also give an

important signal to the reader that a significant qualification is coming, or it may simply slow down the text so the reader can have a moment to absorb what has been said before receiving new information. Make sure every word is necessary to communicate your meaning. If it isn't: delete.

Some Personal Tips
Make your own list of things to watch out for. Each item may do the job when it is needed, but certain words seem to multiply on their own spreading throughout a draft. Weed them out. My list:

ing	Can I take it out and make my writing more direct?
ly	Is this adverb necessary?
that	Sometimes it seems as if each sentence has a *that* and some have two or three. I cut every one I can.
would	Most of my *woulds* add nothing to my text. I subtract them.
very	One of the amazing things about our language is that *very* is usually less rather than more. "It was a very beautiful sunset" is not as beautiful as "It was a beautiful sunset."
quite	One editor claimed I had at least one *quite* on every page of a book manuscript. She was right. They were zapped.

Make your own list and act on it while tuning your draft.

Spel Koreclie
Researchers promise me that the ability to spell correctly is *not* related to intelligence. I am grateful. I am a poor speller, and so are many other writers. Unfortunately, teachers, bosses, editors, readers equate intelligence with spelling. When they see one word misspelled they begin to sneer at the writer. I hate sneers. To avoid them I have several solutions:

1. Marry someone who is a good speller as I did. Marriage may seem like an enormous price to pay for correct spelling. I think it is worth it. Perhaps you can find a friend who will check your spelling without demanding a ring and a mortgage.

2. I have a spell checker on my computer and, boy, do I use it. But it has some problems. The computer is dumb. If a

word is spelled correctly, the computer does not care if it is the right word. Examples: *to* and *too, their* and *there.* And on top of that, my poor spelling combined with my poor typing produces words the spell checker cannot find.

3. I have *The Word Book* beside my typewriter. Mine is published by Houghton Mifflin, but there are similar books on the market. Mine simply has the 40,000 most frequently used words in our language listed alphabetically. I use it every day I revise. If it does not have the word I need to check, I go to my large dictionary.

4. If I can't find the word—*pneumonia* should start with an *n* but it doesn't—I go to *The Bad Speller's Dictionary.* Mine is published by Random House but other publishers have their own versions. It has the wrong spelling followed by the correct one: *neumonia —pneumonia.*

5. I have a list of commonly misspelled words and you should have your own.

Seperate, separate
Lead, led
Its, it's
There, they're, their
To, too
Your, you're
Lose, loose
Occurred
Than, then
Affect, effect
Principle, principal
Can not, cannot

And I find that when I'm writing quickly I can hear one word and write down a sound-alike word, a homonym: *altar* instead of *alter, complement* instead of *compliment, conscience* for *conscious, desert* for *dessert, hear* for *here, know* for *no;* and I have to clear those howlers out of my final draft.

And rules may help; *Lice: i* before *e* except after *c.* Thus, *believe, receive.* The important thing is to make your own list and prop it up in front of you when you tune your final draft.

The Dictionary

The dictionary is as essential a tool to the writer as the hammer is to the carpenter. In the dictionary the meanings of words are recorded. The dictionary is the referee that makes the call, most of the time, on whether the writer is using the right word to communicate meaning.

There are many fine dictionaries but I will demonstrate how the dictionary helps me by an example from *The American Heritage Dictionary of the English Language,* which I keep near my desk.

Since we are talking about words, I look up *word.*

word (wûrd) *n.* 1. *Abbr. wd.* A sound or a combination of sounds, or its representation in writing or printing, that symbolizes or communicates a meaning and may consist of a single morpheme or of a combination of morphemes. 2. Something that is said; an utterance, remark or comment: *May I say a word about that?* 3. *Plural* A discourse or talk; speech. 4. *Plural* The text of a vocal musical composition; lyrics. 5. An assurance or promise; sworn intention: *a man of his word.* 6. a. A command or direction; an order: *executed at the general's word.* b. A verbal signal; a password or watchword. 7. a. News: *the latest word.* b. Rumor: *Word has she's married.* 8. a. *Plural.* A dispute or argument; a quarrel. b. A quarrelsome remark or conversation: *Words were exchanged between umpire and batter.* 9. *Capital* W. a. The Logos. b. The Scriptures or Gospel: *the Word of God. -at a word.* In immediate response. *-by word of mouth.* Orally; by speech. *-have no words for.* To be unable to describe or talk about. *-in a word.* In most precise form; in short: *You are, in a word, a fool. -in so many words.* Precisely as stated; exactly. *-take at one's word.* To be convinced of another's sincerity and act in accordance with his statement. *-word for word.* In the same words. *-tr.v. worded, wording, words.* To express in words. [Middle English *word.* Old English *word.* See *wer-6* in Appendix.]

What does that formal, scholarly, legalistic entry tell me?

First, that there is such a word in our language as *word* and that it is spelled *w–o–r–d.* I am a terrible speller and use the dictionary most often to correct my spelling.

In parentheses, I am told how to pronounce *word* and if I don't understand such marks ^, there is an appendix in the dictionary to tell me the meaning of such signs. It also tells me that word is a noun (*n.*) and what is the proper abbreviation for word (*wd.*).

Then the dictionary tells me the meanings of the word in order of their normal frequency or, to put it another way, the most likely way the word will be understood by a reader. But what's that stuff about "morphemes"? I dunno. I'm a writer and I've heard the word but all I can think of is the morphine I enjoyed during my bypass operation. What do I do?

I look it up in the dictionary: "A linguistic unit of relatively stable meaning that cannot be divided into smaller meaningful parts, as words such as *man* or *most,* or word elements such as *-ly* or *al-* as found in *manly* and *almost.*"

Ah, now I understand.

The dictionary gives me a great range of meanings that may help me use the word properly and closes with a brief history of the word.

What if your use of the word isn't in the dictionary? I might write of someone who talks too much: "I was worded by Tom" or "Tom worded me." The language grows and changes. If, in my opinion after reconsideration, *worded* was the best way to describe his talkativeness and if my editors approved, that might stay in my copy, although it isn't in the dictionary and if it caught on, it might make the next edition of the dictionary. I don't think *worded* as I used it here is accurate enough. I would cut it—I think. It's always a judgment call based on the context. If I used *worded* in dialogue to reveal the way a person used the language incorrectly, then, of course, its usage would be "correct."

The Thesaurus

And what about the thing that is called a thesaurus and credited to Mr. Roget? It is a popular gift for students going to college and most word-processing computer programs even include a thesaurus.

I confess to having a copy of *Roget's Thesaurus* but I just got up to look for it and couldn't find it. I don't remember using it since my freshman year in college. A thesaurus lists all the possible alternative words to the word you look up *without any definitions.* The words with a similar meaning are called synonyms and the ones with opposite meanings may also be included and they are called antonyms, but without definitions you can be fooled into thinking *similar* means *same*. Of course, it doesn't. Each word has its own meaning, and the inexperienced writer can choose a high falutin' word he or she doesn't understand to impress someone and end up looking foolish.

I had been using the program WordPerfect on my computer for years and had never looked to see if it had a thesaurus. It does, and when I look up *word* I am given nineteen nouns and four verbs to choose from: "nouns—*term, expression, statement, utterance, charge, command, mandate, order, gossip, hearsay, rumor, communication, information, message, report, assurance, guarantee, pledge, promise;* verbs—*couch, express, phrase, style.*"

I can imagine a student revising a paper, seeing that word has been used many times, remembering that the instructor has criticized using the same word too often and when coming to a new sentence that says, "The official word from the Reagan administration on El Salvador was . . . ," clicking the thesaurus and inflating the diction by writing, "The official utterance from . . ." or, "The official mandate from . . ." that would make the text sound fancier but would not communicate the meaning intended by the original statement. I would hope the student would not turn the sentence on its head and write, "The Reagan Administration couched its position on El Salvador . . ." but I have seen worse from students infected with thesauritis.

If you use a thesaurus, be sure to look up the meaning of the word you choose.

Revising the Line

After the word comes the line, that unit of writing that may—or may not—become a sentence. The line is that unit of words which surround *the* word, that set off and display the word, and in which two words can ignite to create a meaning that is beyond either of them alone.

Apply the check list to your draft, concentrating on the line:

Is the line specific?
Is the line true?
Is the line mine?

Does the line fit?
Is the line clear?
Will the reader read?
Does the line advance the meaning?
Does the line use tradition?
Does the line flow?

The effective writer has mastered the line in all of its forms. It is the line that provides the energy for each piece of writing, it propels the material and the reader forward.

The Phrase

The phrase is the unit of words that connects the single word to other words so that the phrase creates meaning. It always confused me in school that we studied vocabulary then leapt to the sentence. I usually wrote in small units of words as much as with a single word. I now know I was right, we write with phrases, those small units of language in which words collide and give off a meaning that is different than either word alone. In writing, two and two can make seven or eleven.

The writer is forever excited by what happens when words interact with one another igniting a thought, a feeling, a vision, an insight in the mind of the reader. Perhaps because this New Englander experienced a flash flood in New Mexico, I have forever been fascinated by the energy given off by those two words: *flash flood.* They create an accurate and terrifying picture and their music underscores the meaning. Say the words aloud and hear their hard-edged quickness. They sound like a flash flood.

In revising, I like to focus at important points in my text on those small collections of words that release so much of the energy in writing. Let's look at the first sentence in this section, an undistinguished but workmanlike piece of writing, to examine the small units of language I focused on in revising the sentence. I've cut out the connective words to focus on the key phrases.

The phrase is	This announces that a definition is on its way.
the unit of words that	A bit awkward but I must keep it open to a variety of forms.

connects the single word to other words	Simple, direct, sets what happens in an active manner.
so that	Transitional phrase that should not call attention to itself.
phrase creates meaning.	It is active and direct, saying what the phrase does. The emphasis is on the last word: *meaning.*

At the center of language is the phrase that captures an idea or a mood, but there are some dangers the writer has to guard against. The phrase has so much power that politicians and advertising agencies have become skillful at the glib phrase that sounds good and says little. Our presidential campaigns are no longer debates in which issues are explored but "sound bite" (an interesting phrase in itself) skirmishes in which fragments of language are hurled between candidates. Apart from the issue of abortion, no one can deny the advantage anti-abortion forces gained when they established themselves as being "pro-life." Their opponents, not willing to be "pro-death," rushed to establish their position as being "pro-choice." These phrases oversimplify a complex human/political/theological/medical issue.

Pay attention to the way words rub against each other. In writing, two and two can make five, seven, three, zero.

The Fragment

Formal instruction in writing commands: no sentence fragments. But today's writers qualify that edict: Don't use sentence fragments that don't work. (Watch out for double negatives: Use sentence fragments that work.)

A fragment is a nonsentence: "Tom and John in pickup. Gone fishing." To be a sentence, it should read, "Tom and John hopped into the pickup to go fishing." *But* if the previous sentence read, "The private investigator watched, then scribbled in his notebook, 'Tom and John in pickup. Gone fishing,'" then the fragment would be correct. If you write a sentence fragment and it must remain that way, keep it.

The Clause

The clause contains a noun and a verb and when placed within a sentence extends, deepens, qualifies, enriches the meaning of the sentence. The clause may be set off by commas or may be embedded in the sentence without punctuation. A sentence may not have any clauses or it may have many, whatever is required to develop and clarify the writer's meaning.

The Sentence

The sentence communicates meaning. The previous sentence is an example of the simple, direct subject (*sentence*), verb (*communicates*), object (*meaning*) sentence that is the fundamental building block of English prose.

Sometimes people think the more complex the sentence, the more impressive the mind behind it. Not true. Build your prose with the subject-verb-object sentence, developing it with clauses as you develop your meaning, but return to it at times of confusion to clarify and emphasize. The sentence communicates meaning.

Notes for the Writer Revising the Line

Now I am going to invite you to visit my workroom and allow you to hear the messages I mutter and mumble to myself as I revise the line.

How Many Words Should There Be in a Line?

Well, if I hear correctly, paying attention to the arts of communication as I understand them, and, of course, to the parameters of language usage, it is not, however, just a matter of correctness, but has socioeconomic components as well, that I would advise the writer to cut what can be cut.

Cut what can be cut. Cutting is one of the great satisfactions of revision. Eliminate the unnecessary and the necessary runs free.

Short or Long?

Short for emphasis—"Jesus wept"—with the longer sentences in between. That's my first rule. Let the sentence roll along when that is appropriate to the idea; allow what is being said to determine how it is being said.

And I need to remember to vary my sentence length and design so that I create an attractive—and appropriate—pattern of prose that unrolls before the reader's eye and ear in an interesting fashion.

Finding the Point of Emphasis
The greatest point of emphasis is usually at the end of the line, the next at the beginning. Move the most important piece of information you want to communicate around within the sentence until you hear where it has the greatest impact.

Writing with Metaphors
Robert Frost said, "Poetry is metaphor, saying one thing and meaning another, saying one thing in terms of another." And so is all lively writing prose or poetry. He is a nut; the exam bulldozed me; we had a ball. This is the pure magic in language. By metaphor we liven, illuminate, communicate; the reader reads a metaphor and sees, in an instant, what we mean, how we feel.

Parallelism
If I have a pattern, if I arrange words so they reveal, if I want my reader to build toward a conclusion that will seem inevitable, then the pattern of my words, in this case my clauses, must work in parallel, repeating the pattern that I have established in the beginning. If I have a pattern, if I arrange words so they reveal, if the reader builds toward a conclusion . . . . The first sentence is parallel; the second is not, slipping from first person to second person. When you read it aloud you should hear the writer grind gears.

Listen for the Beat
The line, in all it forms, has a beat. It is not a metronome beat, an even regularity, but a beat that reflects the meaning of the draft. Listen to that beat, then play to it with the choice of words, the length of the line, the pattern of emphasis in the line.

Two Steps Forward, One Step Back
The phrase within the line allows us to qualify, limit, explain. I particularly like to drop a serious note into a humorous

line or a humorous note into a serious line. It keeps the reader listening and clarifies the meaning—or I wouldn't use it.

"I knew how writing should be taught—the opposite of how it was not being learned—when I was in high school. I told them but they didn't listen until I became a consultant. Each time I raised my rates, more listened—to what I said when I was an impertinent eleventh-grader." See how much fun I had writing that, moving forward and back.

Adding Surprise

I write to be surprised. In the sentences about what I knew—and know—about teaching writing, I was surprised by what I wrote. I was also surprised by the "and know" that popped into the last sentence as I was writing it. Those two words connected past and present, quickly and firmly. I find the line, if I write loosely enough, listening to what I do not mean to say, will surprise me, and the best surprises, sharpened and developed, will surprise the reader.

What Comes Before; What Follows

Writing the line I have developed triple vision. I am aware of what I am writing, what came just before, what may be written next. The line grows out of what I have written and grows into what will be written next.

Transitions

Some editors and teachers like transitions—meanwhile back at the ranch—but I try not to write them. Most formal transitions mean that I do not have the material where the reader needs it. If I manage to answer the reader's questions *when they are asked,* I will not have to write transitional phrases.

Pass the Machete, Please

One of the great satisfactions of revision is cutting through the twisted tangle of lines that wind back on themselves, hiding the intended meaning and blocking the way of the reader. Some of the solutions:

- Cut what can be cut.
- Try one simple subject-verb-object sentence.
- Try two or three subject-verb-object sentences.

- Make it more specific.
- Use simpler words and *active* verbs.
- Try a list (as I have done here).

Pronouns

Make sure the *he* relates to a *he*, the *she* to a *she*, *it* to an *it*, and make sure they send the reader back to the right person or thing. It's easy to slip while writing and easy to fix while revising.

Sexist Language   If we say "he" meaning everyone who is a writer, a diplomat, a teacher, an athlete, we exclude the majority sex. If we switch all *he's* to *she's,* we attempt to correct the sins of the past but create new ones. It is easy to get rid of sexist—and racist—language if you eliminate any words that are offensive to readers of a particular gender or background and if you use plurals or specific names so that you do not have to attempt the generic *he.*

- When the writer revises, *he* has an opportunity to clarify *his* meaning.
- When writers revise, *they* have an opportunity to clarify *their* meaning.
- When the writer revises, *he or she* has an opportunity to clarify *his or her* meaning.
- Revision provides the writer with the opportunity to clarify meaning.

Ifs, Ands, *and* Buts

And it is all right to use *and, if, but* to start a sentence or paragraph if that is the most effective way to do it. Don't fall into a repetitive pattern of lines; use different ways of writing a sentence making sure each one serves a reader.

Starting with a Dependent Clause   While trying to make a complex idea clear, it is important to write sentences that run clear and fast. As you can see from the previous section, the reader has to hold the first clause that is dependent on what follows until the rest of the sentence is read, then snap it into place. Sometimes it is appropriate to begin a sentence with a dependent clause for emphasis, transition, or a change of pace, but watch it. For example, "It is important to write sentences that run clear and fast while trying to make a complex idea clear."

Maintaining the Tense

In revising I notice that I *say* I am going to do something and in the same line use *said*. Make sure that your tenses agree. To what? To each other and to the draft's relationship to what is being reported. I like to write in the present tense whenever possible because it is lively and immediate but I can only do it when what I am writing about makes it possible.

Leaving the Reader Dangling

Don't. The reader doesn't like to dangle. It's uncomfortable and confusing. Here's an example of a dangling modifier:

> Writing this book, the editor told me to be clear.

When *writing this book* dangled, it led the reader to connect *writing this book* with the editor. But the editor didn't write this book—I did.

Running On and On and On

It sure does, doesn't it. When I read my own sentences and start to run out of breath, I chop them up and give my readers a chance to breathe.

Punctuation

I once had a writing professor, Carroll Towle, who said to use commas when the reader has to breathe. This rule helped, but it was a little too simple. Brock Dethier tells his corporate executive students, "A comma says 'take a small breath'; a semicolon says, 'another independent clause is coming'; a colon says, 'here comes a list, definition, or explanation.'"

Punctuation is largely a matter of meaning; punctuate to make your meaning clear.

Dashes, Brackets, Parentheses

The dash has been frowned on by grammarians—if you are writing for one don't use it—but I find it is a wonderful device to use to interrupt your line to comment on what you have just written. You can use dashes and parentheses to give information the reader needs at the moment, to qualify and emphasize. Brackets can be used to provide information within quoted material or to parenthesize within parentheses. I delight in the use of dashes, brackets, and parentheses.

Be Spontaneous

John Kenneth Galbraith, an economist who is known for his lively writing on complex economic issues, once said:

> In my own case there are days when the result is so bad that no fewer than five revisions are required. However, when I'm greatly inspired, only four revisions are needed before, as I've often said, I put in that note of spontaneity which even my meanest critics concede.

I am most spontaneous while revising the line. Now that I have my meaning I can make it dance, grump, growl, preach, or just be simple and clear—whatever is appropriate to my subject. One of the greatest joys in writing is revising the line, becoming, through revision, fresh and spontaneous.

Revising the Paragraph

I owe the late Hannah Lees an enormous debt. We had the same agent, and when I met her and discussed the problems I was having with my first magazine articles she suggested I cut my typewriter paper in half and write one paragraph to a page. I followed her advice. I began to learn how to craft the paragraph, the basic rhetorical unit that carries meaning to the reader. This is, I believe, my twentieth book but a book is nothing but a long series of paragraphs; the book is built, like a brick wall, a paragraph at a time.

I revise by making sure, paragraph by paragraph, that I am delivering meaning to my reader in a voice the reader will hear and understand.

The Extended Paragraph

I wanted to call this section "the chunk" because the term *paragraph* seemed too restrictive. Some of my "paragraphs" are verses of poetry; some in my fiction—and even in my nonfiction—are small scenes with dialogue, action and reaction, setting; others are anecdotes, the small narratives so common in popular nonfiction. As you read this section, realize that sometimes the paragraph is only one sentence long and other times it grows beyond the typical paragraph into a longer unit designed to carry meaning to the reader.

Apply the check list to all forms of the paragraph in your draft:

Is the paragraph specific?
Is the paragraph true?
Is the paragraph mine?
Does the paragraph fit?
Is the paragraph clear?
Will the reader read?
Does the paragraph advance the meaning?
Does the paragraph use tradition?
Does the paragraph flow?

Notes for the Writer Revising the Paragraph
Here are some of the thoughts that run through my mind as I fine-tune my paragraphs.

The Topic Sentence
Avoid it. Each paragraph has to have a topic but most paragraphs should not announce it. That insults the reader and slows down the text.

Long Paragraphs or Short
Most of my paragraphs are short.

This does not delight everybody. Many academics feel my paragraphs are too short, and some feel that's true of my words and my sentences. My first textbook was turned down by one publisher because "It will be read for enjoyment, not instruction." I am charged with writing "journalistic" paragraphs, and I was certainly influenced by writing for newspapers where five lines of typewritten prose become ten lines in print. I can and do write long paragraphs in my novels, articles, and textbooks when I need the space to develop my ideas, when I think the audience will be interested enough to read long paragraphs, and when I know the text will fill a full page.

I deliver small loads of information and develop my ideas over a series of paragraphs when other writers would develop the same material in one paragraph. The goal, however, is not to follow a specific paragraph length requirement but to develop and deliver information and ideas in a well-tuned voice.

You should not write in one-length paragraphs but in a pleasing and effective variety of paragraph lengths, normally using shorter paragraphs for emphasis or clarity of complex ideas, longer ones for what carries the reader to and away from those peaks of meaning.

And if your editor, teacher, or the design of the publication in which you are published requires longer or shorter paragraphs, deliver them.

Developing the Paragraph

The old-fashioned instruction, CUE—coherence, unity, and emphasis, is not often taught these days but it is one high-school instruction I remember and try to follow.

Unity: Everything in the paragraph should be about one thing.
Coherence: One thing should logically lead to the next.
Emphasis: The main point of the paragraph should be clear.

Attribution

The reader should be given the source of significant, controversial, or unexpected information. This can be done in many ways. It may be obvious from the text above, it may be gracefully woven into the text, it may be delivered in an announcing or attribution line, it may be cited in a footnote. You should try, however, to do it in such a way that it does not draw the reader's attention away from the information the reader needs.

Opening Paragraphs

The most important paragraph in any draft is the first one. It attracts the reader, establishes the subject, the tone, the form, the length, and the pace of the draft. It is vital to fine-tune the opening paragraph that sets the standard for all the paragraphs that follow.

Descriptive Paragraphs

Description—and I mean description of an idea, theory, process as well as a physical description—is a major function of paragraph crafting. It is important to work from a single angle of vision and show everything in relation to the dominant impression created by the angle of vision. I also like to use the word *reveal,* to remind me to allow the subject to reveal itself in a way natural to the subject. Here is an example of description:

The class watched as the professor with huge glasses, tiny rodent-like mouth, and brown coat sweater scurried into the classroom and dumped a pile of books on the desk, then trotted out. In a minute he was back with more books; then off to return with a third load. He carefully built a three-sided fort of books, took a safe position behind his scholar wall and began, "Chaucer was . . . ."

Dialogue

Dialogue is easy. It is action. "Get thee to a nunnery." When Hamlet says that to Ophelia, he is committing an action against her, and she has to react by going to a nunnery or saying, "Shove off, Hamlet. I'm going to a rock concert with Boris."

Then he answers, "Not Boris."

And she says, "Yes, Boris and I intend . . . ."

Dialogue is constructed from the interaction of characters. Usually, each person's speech is a separate line or paragraph. Dialogue is lively, revealing, fun to write, and fun to read. It shows more than it tells.

Closing Paragraphs

Almost as important as the opening ones. This is what the reader will remember most. In general, I try not to tell the reader what to think or feel in the last paragraph, but to give information that will make him or her think or feel.

Using Typography To Make Meaning Clear

The extended paragraph should include typographical devices that made meaning clear. The computer and the development of desktop publishing has multiplied the typographical options available to the writer. Some of the devices a writer may consider include:

1. *To clarify.* Break up the text as we have with headings that usually indicate a new section. Indented subheads can indicate even smaller units of meaning. Usually the heads have a coherent and consistent system to show their importance, using capital letters and small letters; underlining, bold-face, and italics. Sometimes the sections are numbered with roman numerals, arabic numbers, and letters that allow the writer's outline to show and help the reader understand

the organization of complex material and to be able to refer to it efficiently.

2. *To emphasize.* It is important that the reader know your central message and the material on which it is built. This can be done with an indented list of the main points, often single spaced if the text is double spaced. The writer may also use bold-face, underlining, and capital letters to call attention to the most significant parts of the text.

3. *To visualize.* With the increase in the use of sophisticated computers, more and more writers are able to clarify and emphasize with graphs, charts, and increasingly clever forms of graphic communication.

Revising the Draft

Company's coming! Run through and put the dishes in the clothes hamper, the laundry in the trunk of the car, make the bed, swish out the shower, fluff up the pillows on the sofa. Now, at the end of the revision process, read through the draft quickly with the following questions in mind to make the copy as clean and readable as possible.

Is the draft specific?
Is the draft true?
Is the draft mine?
Is the draft clear?
Will the reader read?
Does the draft use tradition?
Does the draft flow?

Suggestion

Take a draft and read through it four times. Tedious? It shouldn't be because you will be rewarded with little surprises of insight and understanding along the way. Apprehensive? Scared? Afraid you'll make a mistake? Don't be. You aren't so much trying to make the draft correct as tuning your voice so it will rise clear and strong from the page.

9

Rewriting Is Writing

But what will happen if I don't have time for such extensive revision?

All the revision you do will improve your first drafts. Just one intense experience with the craft of revision will change the way you write. And the more you revise, the more you will discover that you are rewriting *before* you write and *while* you write.

Rewriting Before Writing

When I began to study the writing process and write about it, I saw the process in three clear stages: prewriting, writing, rewriting. But the more I learned, the more blurred the borders of each stage became; I found myself performing last-stage language tasks before my first draft, prewriting on the final draft. Process was a helpful way to examine the writing process—if I didn't take it too seriously. Then my writing was studied by Dr. Carol Berkenkotter of Michigan Technological

University and I discovered with her that much of my prewriting is rewriting. Experienced writers are rewriting before they write the first page and as they write the draft.

How Rewriting Affects Planning

The experienced rewriter anticipates problems while planning what to write next. And the anticipated problem can often be solved in advance—I rewrite before writing. Here are some of the ways I prewrite or plan and how I may identify a problem in advance because of my rewriting experience.

Planning Method

1. I receive an assignment and study it to see the central problem that must be solved, then list solutions.

■ I may decide that the problem of a particular assignment is tone, another organization. Each problem creates its own agenda of possible solutions. And each solution may come with its own problems. If the solution is to write nostalgically of the past, how do I involve readers who were not alive then? If I organize by narrative, how can I weave in technical information the reader needs? I must also find and try a solution or approach that can be accomplished under the assignment's conditions of length and deadline. ■

2. I draft the title of the nonfiction book, chapter, or article, then write all the subheads for the smaller units of the piece. This shows me what has to be covered, when, and at what length.

■ I can see the pattern of the piece of writing, the sequence of writing problems I must solve. This allows me to revise the pattern so that I face problems I think I will be able to solve under the conditions that will govern the writing. In this chapter I talk about rewriting BEFORE writing, rewriting WHILE writing, and revisiting the entire writing process. ■

3. I fastwrite a quick and sloppy draft, what Calvin Trillin calls a "vomit all" and I call a discovery draft to see where my writing is taking me.

■ Once I have a rough map of the territory I have to explore I can see the crevices, the quicksand, the cliff faces I should avoid and the trail I should try. ■

4. I write the title, the opening paragraph, the three to five main points that will get me to the end—which I try to sketch.

■ This establishes the voice, pace, and direction of the draft. If it reveals problems I know I cannot solve in the writing, at least under the conditions of this writing task, I start with another version of this sketch. I have discovered my problems without having taken the time and exerted the effort to produce a draft. ■

5. I find a line, a fragment of language, that contains the central tension of a piece of writing.

■ That seed reveals what I have to do to complete the draft, the same way that a plant seed will tell my wife the type of care she will have to provide to cultivate the plant. The tension in that key line will tell me a great deal about what I will have to go through for the idea to grow from one line to a book. ■

These are all examples of rewriting before writing. There are many other ways to plan and I will sometimes use some of them—the formal academic outline complete with roman numerals, arabic numbers, capital and small letters; the screenwriter's story-board technique in which each element is listed on a separate three-by-five-inch card and arranged into a working order; the trip-planning approach in which you write the ending, the destination, then go back to the beginning and create the map of how to get to the destination—but all of them will be much more effective if you have the experience with which to perceive writing problems—and solutions—in advance.

Rewriting While Writing

I also find that I am rewriting as I write. This may mean, of course, that I worry a sentence into being or fix a problem when I see it, for example, spotting the need to define a term and defining it immediately. There is a danger in this. I am a believer in fastwriting. Get the first draft down at top speed, outrunning the censor and causing the accidents of language and insight that are vital for effective writing.

Many times I get around this problem by maintaining the flow and marking a spot that will need reworking later by underlining, putting it in boldface, enclosing it in brackets, or inserting a note to myself that I will see when rewriting the draft. There are, however, two techniques I find myself using in which I rewrite while writing.

Chunking

The computer allows me to write, then rewrite, in chunks. I often write five to eight paragraphs in a burst, then go back to develop them, cutting, adding, moving around, polishing. I go over the entire draft later, of course, but I do less revision when I have "chunked" the draft.

I do not do it all the time because it often keeps me from encouraging the flow of language that is vital for me.

Layering

Another technique I have been using, especially in writing fiction, is to create a draft by layers. This method is also ideally suited for the computer. I start each day at the beginning of the chapter and write over what I have written the day before. Each day the draft grows longer and more deeply developed as I create another layer of text. I respond to the problems that seem most immediate at the time and if I'm not responding effectively to one problem, I move to another. I'll come back to it tomorrow or the day after. Obviously this technique only works if you have disciplined yourself to start well ahead of deadline.

I continue to learn to write and I hope you will as well. Tonight this book is done and I will start work on another. As I begin my next book, the following instructions to myself stand by my computer:

- *Nulla dies sine linea.* Never a day without a line.
- Work at the edge, beyond where you have written before. Write what you cannot yet write.
- Break long writing projects into achievable, daily units.
- Seek the line that contains the central tension of the draft.
- Lower your standards until you are able to write. Create, then criticize.
- Write fast to outrun the censor and create essential accidents of insight and language.
- Establish a priority but write many things. When one doesn't go another will.
- Write out loud to hear the instructive voice of the evolving text.
- Reveal the subject to yourself with specific details.
- Do not strain: listen, receive, play.

Index

A

Accuracy, 150
    Contextual, 115–116
    Factual, 114–115
Active voice, 156
Anecdote, 119
Answers, without questions, 60
Assignment, 41
Attribution, 126–128, 171
Audience, 13, 19, 61, 73–85
    Ask reader's questions, 79–80
    Empathy, 77–78
    Evidence for reader, 78
    Expectation, 96–97
    Identify reader, 74–75
    Language for reader, 78
    Reader's world, 75–78
    Satisfaction, 113
    Test Readers, 80–85
    Write to one other reader, 75
    Write to yourself, 74–75
    Writing for bad readers, 81
Authority, 28, 113, 119
Awareness, 6–7, 40, 121–122

B

Beginning a new writing
    project, 28–31
Bibliography, 124–125
Bleak House, 89
Boston Globe, 15, 16, 23, 27,
    56–57
Bracket, 168
Brainstorming, 16
but, 167

C

Caro, Robert, 150
Carver, Raymond, 2

Chunking, 177
Clarity, 151, 172
Clause, 164
    Dependent, 167
Cliche, 155
Code word, 52
Column, Boston Globe, 15
Communication, 8–9
Community of writers, 83–84
Connection, 7, 117–118
Cormier, Robert, 6, 41
Craft
    Of revision, 10–11
    Pleasure of, 9–10
Critic
    Responding to, 83
    Silencing, 43
Cut, 60–61, 69, 103, 166–167
    Unnecessary words,
        156–157

D

D'Alfonso, Gerald, 16
Dangling, 168
Dash, 168
Daybook, 16, 35
Demonstration, 17–20, 23–25,
        35–36, 45, 56–57, 91–95,
        105, 107–108, 147–148
Definition, 155
Design
    Form, 97–102
    Structure 108–111
Detail
    Descriptive, 119
    Revealing, 32–33, 52–53,
        117
Dethier, Brock, 168
Development, 61–62, 171

DeVries, Peter, 2
Dialogue, 172
    With draft, 55
Dickens, Charles, 89
Dictionary, 159–160
Didion, Joan, 2, 38–39, 44
"Digging," Seamus Heaney,
        145–146
Dillard, Annie, 48
Discovery, 4–5, 18, 42, 87–97
    Form, 87–97
    Structure, 104–108
Distance, 70–71
    Close-ups 70–71
    Step-back, 71
    Zoom, 71
Distracting material, 67
Documentation, 110, 112–131
Draft
    Discovery, 42
    To explore, 11, 18, 26
    Instructs, 62–63, 85
    Revising, 173

E

Edge, 178
Elbow, Peter, 42
Empathy, 77–78
Emphasis, 165, 172
Endings, 45–46, 110, 172
Evidence, 14, 20–21, 62, 78,
        112–131
Exploration, 4, 18, 23–47
    Attitude, 26–28
    Continuing, 47–48
    Starting, 42–47
    Where, 39–41
    In writing, 31–39
Eye, 31–32

F

Fact, 119
Fairness, 11
Fast writing, 42–43, 178
Faulkner, William, 43, 48
Fitzgerald, F. Scott, 42–43
Flaubert, Gustav, 150
Flow, 152
Focus, 30, 64–72, 109
    Distance, 70–71
    Frame, 68–69
    Leads, 66
    Questions to reveal focus,
        65–68
    Say one thing, 65–68
        How find, 65
        Importance of, 72
    Sharpen, 66
    Titles, 66
    What to keep in, 69
    What to leave out, 69
Form, 58, 86–111
    Designing form, 97–102
    Discovering form,
        87–97, 98
    Excluding 103
    External form, 89–91
    Including, 102–103
    Internal form, 87–88
Fowles, John, 27
Fragment, 163
Frame, 68–69
Frost, Robert, 165

G

Galbreath, John Kenneth,
    32–33, 169
Goodman, Ellen, 2

H

Haygood, Wil, 150
Heaney, Seamus "Digging,"
    145–146
Hemingway, Ernest, 48
Hollander, John, 43
Horace, 47
Housman, A.E., 150
Howell, Mort, 18

I

if, 167
Image, 33, 53, 61
Imagination, 41
Information, 58,
    Basic forms of, 119–120
    Importance of, 112–114
    Qualities of, 114–119
    Where to find, 120–128
    Writing with, 128–123
-ing, 157
Interview, 40, 122–123

J

Jargon, 155–156
Johnson, Bob, 1

K

Kafka, Franz, 8
Kramer, Evelynne, 15

L

Language, see Voice
Layering, 177

Lead, 16, 44–45, 60, 109, 171, 176
  For Focus, 66
Length, 43, 170–171
Lees, Hannah, 169
Libraries, 39–40, 123–124
Line, 15, 16, 34–39, 60, 178
  Appearance, 35–38
  Definition, 35
  Encourage, 37
  Revising, 161–162
  Sound, 38
  Tension, 35–36
Lively writing, 113–114
-ly, 157

M

Malamud, Bernard, 3, 10
McBride, Mekeel, 17, 150
McHugh, Heather, 8
Meaning, 12, 18–19, 58, 61, 151
Memory, 5–6, 40, 121
Metaphors, 165
Michelangelo, 88
Minnie Mae, 15, 16, 17
Morrison, Toni, 2, 150
Mozart, 95
Music, 8, 53–54

N

Newkirk, Tom, 84
Note-taking, 125–126
Noun, 129–130, 156
nulla dies sine linea, 47, 178

O

Observation, see Awareness
Olds, Sharon, 150
Openings, 16, 44–45, 66. 109
Order, 13–14, 20, 61, 86–111
  Designing form, 97–102
  Designing Structure 108–111
  Discovering form, 87–97, 98
  Discovering Structure, 104–108
  External form, 89–91
  Excluding 103
  Including, 102–103
  Internal form, 87–88
Orwell, George, 150, 151
Outline, 16, 43–46, 104–106

P

Pace, 110
Paragraph, 131
  Revising, 169–173
Parallelism, 165
Parenthesis, 168
Pattern, 7–8, 32, 54
Phrase, 53, 130, 162–163
Piercy, Marge, 7
Plagiarism, 126
Plan, 43–46, 175–176
Plato, 9
Pliny, 47
Praise, 83
Pritchard, Marjorie, 90
Problem solving, 3–4, 33–34
Process
  Of revision, 11–17
  Writing, 17–21

Pronouns, 167
Proportion, 110–111
Punctuation, 168

Q

Question, 34, 46
    To reveal focus, 65–66
    Without answer, 60
quite, 157
Quotation, 119

R

Read
    Aloud, 58, 143
    Answers without questions,
        60
    Audience, 61
    Clues to meaning, 53–54
    Code word, 52
    To discover, 12, 18, 49–63
    Evidence, 62
    Fastreading, 50–51
    Form, 58
    Fragments, 52
    Ideas, 61
    Image, 53, 60
    Information, 58
    Instructions from draft,
        62–63
    Leads, 60
    Line, 60
    Meaning, 58, 61
    Music, 53–54
    Order, 61
    Pattern, 54
    Questions for the draft, 51
        Without answers, 60

reader, as a 49–51
Revealing detail, 52–53
Significant phrase, 53
Specifics, 60
Structure, 58
Thread, 54
Voice, 53–54, 58, 62
What isn't written, 54
For what needs work, 59–63
For what works, 55–59
Reader, see Audience
Role play, 50
Readers' questions, 46
Resonance, 117
Revision
    For audience, 13, 19
    Before writing, 174–176
    Checklist 149–173
    Craft of, 147–173
    Feel of, 145–147
    For evidence, 14, 20–21
    Marks, editing, 149
    For meaning, 12–13, 18–19
    For order, 13–14, 20
    Part to whole—and back,
        147–148
    Process, 11–17
    Satisfactions of, 3–10
    For voice, 14–15, 21
    While writing, 177–178
Run on, 168

S

The Saturday Evening Post, 1
Scanlan, Christopher, 17, 150
Sentence, 130–131, 164
    Fragment, 163
Sexist language, 167

Significance, 117–118
Simon, Neil, 3
Singer, Isaac Beshavis, 59–60, 103
Sketch, 46
Specific, revealing, 32–33, 52–53, 58, 60, 116–117, 150, 178
Spelling, 15, 16, 157–158
Spontaneity, 169
Stafford, William, 27, 28
Starobin, Michael, 67
Statistic, 119
Steinbeck, John, 68
Stopping writing, 48
Structure, 58, 86–111
Suggestions, 25, 28, 31, 39, 40, 41, 47, 48, 51, 55, 59, 63, 68, 70, 71, 72, 79, 80, 85, 97, 102, 103, 106, 111, 114, 119, 120, 128, 131, 142, 173
Support, 61–62
    Supporting material, 67
Surprise, 26–27, 42, 144, 166

T

Tappen, Dick, 15
Tense, 168
Tension
    For focus, 65
    In line, 35–37
    Productive, 29–30
Test readers, 80–85
that, 157
Thesaurus, 160–161
Thesis Statement, 91

Thought
    Adventure of, 9
Thread, 54
Time
    Fragments, 47–48
Title, 16, 43–44, 175, 176
    For Focus, 66
To be, 156
Topic, 28–31
    Authority on, 28–29
    Focus on, 30
    Instructs, 30–31
    With productive tension, 29–30
Topic sentence, 91, 170
Towle, Carroll, 168
Tradition, 151–152
    Conscious, 90–91
    Form, 101
    Subconscious, 89–90
Trail, 46
Transitions, 166
Trollope, Anthony, 47
Tuchman, Barbara, 14–15
Turning points, 109–110
Twain, Mark, 152
Typography, 172–173

U

Updike, John, 47

V

Valery, Paul, 47
Velocity, 42–43
Verb, 129–130, 156
very, 157
Visualize, 173

Voice, 8, 14–15, 21, 62,
        132–173
    Definition, 133–134
    Expected, 139–141
    Formal, 139–140
    Hearing your voice,
        132–142
    Importance of, 137–138
    Influences on, 135–136
    Informal, 140
    In line, 38
    Personal, 135–136
    Read, 53–54, 58
    Reader's language, 78
    Sexist, 167
    Of text, 141–142
    Traditional, 139–141

    Tuning, 142–147
    Your language or mine, 137
Vonnegut, Kurt, 67, 69

W

Weldon, Fay, 57
Welty, Eudora, 33
White, E.B., 91, 92, 150
Word, 129–130
    Revising, 152–161
Would, 157
Writing against expectation,
        96–97
Writing process
    Demonstrating, 17–21